The Search Within

Christmas Humphreys

THE SEARCH WITHIN
A Course in Meditation

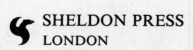

SHELDON PRESS
LONDON

First published in Great Britain in 1977 by
Sheldon Press, Marylebone Road, London NW1 4DU

Printed in Great Britain by
The Camelot Press Ltd, Southampton

ISBN 0 85969 088 1 (cloth)
ISBN 0 85969 089 X (paper)

Christmas Humphreys was born in London and educated at Malvern College and Trinity Hall, Cambridge, where he read Law. He was called to the Bar in 1924, the same year as he founded the Buddhist Lodge of the Theosophical Society, now known as The Buddhist Society. The Buddhist Society, which the author still leads, became independent in 1926 and began to publish its own journal, *The Middle Way*. In 1959 he took Silk and in 1968 became a permanent judge of the Central Criminal Court at the Old Bailey. Since founding The Buddhist Society he has written numerous book and poems about Buddhism and is acknowledged as one of the country's leading authorities on the religion.

CONTENTS

PREFACE

This Course is designed for the use of anyone who is not wedded to any particular school or method in the search for the Self, or Mind, or Essence, or Light within.

It is proffered as a treatment for the whole sick man as distinct from an ointment applied to the skin. It is therefore more than another method of meditation, of which there are a score available in published form.

It is a Course, not a mere miscellany of material grouped under chosen themes. It is not specifically Buddhist, although the Themes and most of the material have emerged in the course of the forty-five years' life of the Zen Class of The Buddhist Society.

The quotations are in no sense offered as authority for what they say. There is no such thing as authority for any spiritual truth save the personal experience of the individual in finding it to be true. In fact, the source of many of the quotations is unknown. At some time they were found and used and re-used, and many are of my own creation based on my own experience.

References are vague, quite often because the actual reference was never known or has been forgotten. Many of the works quoted are available in a dozen translations or editions, and the oft-used phrase, 'From the Pali Canon' represents a small library of volumes of the scriptures of the Theravada school of Buddhism. The enquirer may seek in the publications of the Pali Text Society or the condensed anthology, *Some Sayings of the Buddha*, edited by Woodward and published by The Buddhist Society.

The Bibliography may help the user of the Course to build up a personal library, but the list given is only a tithe of the works in my own library re-read and quoted as seemed helpful.

St John's Wood   T. C. H.
May, 1976

INTRODUCTION

'Even Buddhas do but point the Way.' If this is so, no self-proclaimed or much-sought Teacher can do more.

So with the Search Within, which countless pilgrims have attempted to describe. Each seeks, and each ultimately finds, all treading their own variant of the one Way, from the world of illusion to the world of Reality, and the realization that the two are one.

Yet each can point, and perhaps should point as far as he believes that he can see. If it is well said that 'the West has lost its soul and needs to find it', each nation or group of nations is composed of individuals, and each must seek, and tread the Way, and find what may be found, and none shall save his soul save as he finds the Way, and on it learns to become what he has ever been.

'Modern men', wrote Dr D. T. Suzuki in 1950, 'are always producing or achieving something palpable, something that can be measured by the senses. They have no soul, no centre, no consciousness of an integrating whole within themselves. They have forgotten their Self.'

This work is an exhortation to remember. It is concerned with the long process of Self-finding. True, the Spirit or Self or the Light within is already there, within, but it has to be sought and found, and re-become, and the process is one of self training, self applied.

Hence this Course, born of fifty years of climbing—clambering might be a better word—up this narrow, well-marked but intensely difficult Way. It is not a mere collection of fine sayings, with appropriate comment, like the works of Aldous Huxley and Victor Gollancz. It is meant to be used as a manual, a guide, as suggested by a fellow-pilgrim to those who, too, believe in a Beyond to this 'sorry scheme of things entire' in which, like rats in a cage, we revolve unceasingly. It is therefore not for the scholar, who knows so much 'about it and about' already, nor for the high-brow student already wedded firmly to his own self-chosen Way, and certainly not for those ever ready to prostitute great Wisdom for personal gain.

Rather it is a collection of ordered Themes to be met with and subsumed upon the Way, in one sense with a multitude of seekers, in another vital sense alone. There is here no Teacher, no Personality vibrant with 'charisma' to reveal at last the one and only Truth and to act as Saviour to those who crave for one. Prayer, in the sense of petition to a Force without to save one from the effects of error, has no place in it. As Sir Edwin Arnold wrote in *The Light of Asia.*

> Pray not! the Darkness will not brighten! Ask
>   Nought from the Silence, for it cannot speak! . . .
> Within yourselves deliverance must be sought;
>   Each man his prison makes.

Later we shall see how this utter repudiation of dogma and authority is one of the most remarkable features of Buddhism. To paraphrase it here in the vernacular, 'If a doctrine works in action, use it; if not, ignore it, whoever taught it at any time'.

There is therefore here a minimum of doctrine as such. All emphasis is on the Way and the daily, hourly treading of it. The words are proffered, whoever spoke or wrote them, for their value in action by the individual who studies them, then digests them and finally attempts to apply them to every situation of the day.

Surely study is necessary, that the everyday mind may absorb the idea as given, and raise its habitual consciousness just so much nearer the level on which they dwell. But then they must be digested, and perhaps the most famous process is that of meditation, of which at the moment we hear more and more. But meditation is not a substitute for study. It may help to digest great principles; it does not produce them. Nor will digested principles reveal the Self within, and enable the seeker to merge with it; there must be unceasing application of these Themes or principles or forces, call them what you will, in the endless situations of the daily round, in monastery or public house, in the office, at the bus-stop, in the home.

These Themes are therefore here to be used, intensely and unceasingly, as food for the mind when not otherwise engaged, as principles of action when the next situation arises.

And use them firmly, not flabbily. As R. H. Blyth advised in his *Zen in English Literature*, quoting the famous Master Unmon,

'If you walk, just walk. If you sit, just sit.
But don't wobble!'

Most of those now reading this work have a daily round of earning
a living or running a house, coping with the demands of family and
friends and then, perhaps once or twice a week, attending a meeting
at which deep thoughts are considered, with meditation perhaps to
follow, and so home. This, for the average mind, will achieve very
little. We are all bound in a mass of fixed habits, conclusions,
convictions, choices and determined views, the whole so strong that
an occasional concentration on the Search Within will make no
impact whatsoever. Surely the Theme in use should lie like a cork
held under water, ready to pop up into consciousness whenever there
is no need for mere worldly concentration. As Epictetus, the Stoic
slave of Greece, declared,

> You must know that it is no easy thing for a principle to become
> a man's own unless each day he maintain it and hear it main-
> tained, as well as work it out in life.
>
> Epictetus

This is surely sound. Each of these Themes assumes substantial
work on the preceding ones, and results grow steadily, however
slowly, in raised habitual awareness.

The purpose of the Course is to find the Self, the Self which is at
the same time within/without. This involves, as we shall see, the
rousing and development of the intuition, which in turn involves
abandoning the rigid march of logic in favour of a gentle, soft
absorption of a new idea, perhaps beyond reason, sense and even
credibility, but certainly beyond the formulated bonds of thought.

In the lay-out of the book there has therefore been no attempt to be
logical, consistent or complete. Room has been left for duplication,
contradiction, paradox and humour. It would be presumptuous to
claim that each Theme is a step forward from the last. Truth is a net.
Pick up any point of it and the rest, so to speak, comes up with it in
consciousness. But each and every part has been designed to help to
rouse the intuition into the glorious state of actual experience. After
that, all argument from any source is vain. One *knows*!

The layout of each Theme derives from many a volume of The Buddhist Society's *The Middle Way* which used to end with a page, 'In the Meditation Hour'. The pages open with a Theme. Then come supporting short quotations. Then a poem or two. Then sentences for daily chewing, 'It has been Said'; and finally questions to ask oneself or, if one is bold enough, each other.

Make friends with poetry. It is not a form of prose cut up into lengths, nor need it be ornamented with metre and rhyme. But it is profoundly different from prose, and even more so from the hysterical and unformed rubbish which passes too often today under that honoured name.

Distinguish poetry from verse. Much excellent verse displays, in my opinion, no glimmer of poetry, which may be regarded as light, from bright to brilliant, which illumines a poem, or a verse of one, or even a single line which makes it memorable, and loved by all who appreciate a means of moving nearer to Reality.

But poetry is far more than illumined literature, a splendid craft which blossoms to please the ear and eye. It is of value in this Course because at its best it says what prose cannot. The words are in the same language, though often heightened in effect, but the impact on the reader is very different. A single couplet can say more than a paragraph of prose, and a poem much more than an essay on the subject many times its length. Why? Because it appeals to the heart and the intuition, where prose and much of verse speaks only to the intellect. It says a great deal and far more effectively than words can produce in any other way.

So please read the poems carefully, and slowly, and let the meaning speak to you in its own way. The result will be a profit far greater than the pleasure derived.

The sequence of Themes is shown in the Contents. Use them as you will; one a week, one a month or . . . but it is for the student to decide. It is all hard work and there are no short cuts. All that has been written by fools about the use of drugs for the attainment of enlightenment is evil. Of course there are drugs which produce hallucinations which may be pleasant. So does alcohol in sufficient quantity. No, there are no short cuts in the search within. As Laurens Van Der Post has written, 'Life is its own journey', and it is a long one. Can it be short when, in terms of 'the convenient illusion', time, the universe has already known periods we cannot even pronounce? But if the journey is long, the end, we are told by those who seem to know, is sure; Enlightenment, the return to the source of all that is. For ever? No, say some, but at least for a while. And then? We shall find out. Meanwhile it is enough to know, as we shall soon discover that Browning was right:

Truth is within ourselves; it takes no rise
From outward things, whate'er you may believe.
There is an inmost centre in us all,
Where truth abides in fulness; and around
Wall upon wall the gross flesh hems us in.
         ... 'To *know*'
Rather consists in opening out a way
Whence the imprisoned splendour may escape,
Than in effecting entry for a light
Supposed to be without.

From Paracelsus

CONCENTRATION AND MEDITATION

Once again there is a wave of interest in meditation, and there must be now some hundreds of books on the market dealing with forms of meditation as allegedly practised in India, Japan and Tibet, or Western variations. It was in relation to a sudden interest some forty years ago that the Buddhist Society produced its *Concentration and Meditation* (1935) to raise if possible the standard of motive for this age-long practice. For right motive is vital. Meditation develops considerable power in the mind, and if this new force is used for selfish ends the effect on the individual seems to be disastrous. This is 'black magic' leading to spiritual death. This danger will be referred to in greater detail later.

This is not a text-book on the technique of meditation, but rather material for a self-applied Course for those genuinely interested in spiritual development. As with all its methods and application it concerns the whole strength of the mind turned inward to find the Self, and only then turned outward to apply the Wisdom so gained in the service of all that lives. It is indeed a great adventure.

THE GREAT ADVENTURE

Mind development and control is as well known in the East as machinery is known to Westerners, but to the latter it is a science of which we are as yet on the fringe. Just as the tide, however, on reaching the limits of the ebb turns back, so the extraverted consciousness of the West has all but reached the limits of its outward turning, and is beginning to flow within.

To the Buddhist the mind and its control is all-important. He knows the all-powerful nature of thought, and that character and environment are alike the children of the mind. He knows, too, that so long as the exercise of this all-powerful instrument be used with a pure motive, only time can separate him from his longed-for Goal. That there are difficulties between the student and the perfect use of

7

mind is obvious, for just as the expert player of any game must undergo prolonged and often wearisome preliminary exercises before he is master of his own technique, so the would-be slayer of Avidya (ignorance) must patiently submit to iron self-discipline before the wild horses of thought can be tamed and harnessed to his will. Before the instrument can be used it must be created, but once created it represents the wherewithal for the building up of character and for the enlightenment of all mankind.

Concentration, or mind-control, as distinct from Meditation proper, is only the mental counterpart of physical training, and there is nothing particularly spiritual or mysterious about its practice or technique. It calls for no special hours nor place nor posture, and the only apparatus needed is the daily round. Every successful business or professional man learns to concentrate, but only one in a thousand attempts to bring the mental faculty under the direct control of the will. Hence, however skilled in concentrating on the task in hand, most men find themselves, when not absorbed in any problem, at the mercy of passing thoughts, whether good or evil, and a prey to the 'mass suggestion' of rumour, popular (i.e., Press-made) opinion, and the ready-made views and judgements of their friends.

Yet a trained and disciplined mind under the direct control of the will is a prerequisite for true Meditation, and exercise which is directed to a far higher end, the dissolution of the separated self and the ultimate union of the 'dewdrop' and the 'Shining Sea'. This clear distinction between the creation of the instrument and its use must never be overlooked, for only when a disciplined mind has been successfully directed to the building up of moral character is it safe or wise to embark on meditation, which, while offering far greater rewards, bears corresponding penalties for selfish or improper use.

There is, however, an intermediate exercise, knowledge of which has been brought to the West as 'Meditation on the Breath'. It is best known as one of the fundamental exercises in 'Mindfulness' stressed in the Theravada or Southern School of Buddhism, where it is known as *Anapana-sati*. It may be, however, that it is rather an exercise in Concentration than Meditation in the usual sense of the term, but it is certainly of immense value in creating the instrument to be used in true Meditation.

MEDITATION ON THE BREATH

The essence of the practice is concentration on the actual process of breathing which, after all, goes on all the time. It begins with just watching the breath as it enters and leaves the nostrils, but in time the consciousness becomes one with the actual process of breathing.

Its first use is as an exercise in concentration, negative in that so long as attention is given to the breath one cannot think, feel, want or be concerned with anything *else*. Even ten minutes of such total absorption on a chosen object is an achievement for the beginner, and forty-five minutes at a time is remarkable. Secondly, it has positive value as producing the habit of deep breathing, both in and out, and thus helping general health, especially for the city-dweller in his all too polluted atmosphere. Thirdly, it has symbolic value, for one is consciously breathing in the *prana* or life-force of the universe and giving it back to the universe, mindful of 'suffusion' with all forms of it.

But there comes a point where concentration enters the field of true meditation. Now the mind is involved, although for a while passively. Regular concentration on the breath, which can be carried out anywhere and at any time, begins to reduce the whirlpool of thought-feeling-emotion in which we habitually revolve. The storm subsides, the winds of desire die down. The noise of the world's affray, from naked war to traffic and the senseless chattering of those around one, fades out of consciousness. The mind is progressively stilled.

But thoughts flow in: that forgotten letter, the family worry, the pleasures of the day to come. How shall we cope with them? A hundred ways have been suggested, any one of which will suffice if successful. We are back on negative control, so to focus every faculty on the process of breathing as to allow no other interest or activity to intrude. We must recognize the intrusion, for it is there. But we must learn to let it go, and so revert to the business in hand.

Into this emptiness of any other 'thing' will rise in time repressed contents of the mind, a medley of thoughts, desires, regrets, forgotten duties, and wilfully forgotten guilt. More from the still unconscious field of the mind will come what are now called archetypal images, exciting, majestic, frightening as may be. An example is the repressed function of our twofold mental make-up, as Jung described it, that of thinking versus feeling, according to our type. Have we lived too much in the head or the heart? But then comes, sooner or later, and we must not be impatient, some dim awareness of the Self, the true man, to find which the Zen master Hui-neng said, 'To meditate is to realize inwardly the imperturbability of the Essence of Mind'.

Such is the Meditation on the Breath, and many schools of meditation in fact go no further.

ON SELF-KNOWLEDGE

The student in meditation is apt to meet many difficulties at the outset because the ancient necessity of self-knowledge is not recognized. In his early attempts he experiences a confusion of aims, desires, and ideas which form a resistance in himself from which he may conclude that the Way is not for him, or at least, not yet. Hence the necessity of 'clearing the ground' before one can develop the *capacity* to meditate.

Instead of fighting the chattering urgencies of unwanted thoughts, try admitting them as friends. Repression is futile, for they must and will continually find expression. They have something to tell the student of himself which must be heeded and understood. This clutter of habits and ideas, derived from tradition, education and authority, may or may not be worth taking along the path of regeneration. Their comparative worth and meaning must be carefully examined, and only those retained which are essential to the student's individual path, for only thus can he discover what that path may be.

As he works his way through these accretions, he will find that the body, mind and emotions, *apart from what he has allowed them to become*, have a wisdom of their own. Each is a manifestation of

Spirit, with an essential purpose which it is his business to discover and obey before he can effectively control. Thereafter he works from knowledge, which is clear-seeing, rather than by faith, which gropes in the dark, and this knowledge is the fruit of patient exploration into their essential meaning and dynamic potentialities for *him*.

THE INTUITION

The creative faculty, which is the intuition, is not developed in us but released. As the student progresses further in self-knowledge, he begins to contact it. Instead of having to 'will' himself into deliberate meditation, he finds the way has been made for it to function naturally. Of itself it proceeds to that imaginative reconstruction which must precede external expression. The habit of meditation persists through his daily life, so that he continually receives refreshment and knowledge which, without any apparent mental effort, he is able to apply to life and its problems, shaping them to the pattern of a fair design. He finds he is in touch with a new strength, discovers a new peace and sense of security. Regeneration has begun. He has 'come home'. But not, observe, by moral strain and intellectual effort to acquire and achieve, but by the true relaxation which permits him to 'be'. In short, by 'dropping it', he discovers himself; in losing his life he finds it. But we have to discover what it is we have to drop before the way can be cleared to the One which is the fount of the Multiple, and the first injunction has always been that of Self-knowledge. This implies unremitting effort quite as arduous as the more obvious way of a surface discipline, but the method is different. In the latter the source of strength is the human will, which is useful so long as we recognize its limits, for it is but the *part*. In the former, reason and emotion, reconciled by enlightenment, find their focus in the middle way, from whose summit, the peak of the triangle, both derive. Only when the whole man is thus harmoniously and naturally related, and the consent of all his parts given to the leadership of Spirit, is it able to work for him and through him. Only thus does he contact the profound reality of 'Action in inaction'.

And how shall the 'whole man' be harnessed to this new purpose?

In the Pali Canon is a lovely phrase a thousand times repeated, to live all day and every day 'mindful and self-possessed'. Spoken by the Buddha to his monk-disciples, it applies to all of us all the time.

MINDFUL AND SELF-POSSESSED

And how, brethren, is a brother self-possessed?
Herein, brethren, a brother, both in his going forth and in his homereturning, acts composedly. In looking forward and in looking back he acts composedly. In bending or stretching (arm or body) he acts composedly. In wearing his robes and bearing bowl and robe; in eating, drinking, chewing, swallowing: in relieving nature's needs: in going, standing, sitting, sleeping, waking, speaking, keeping silence, he acts composedly. That, brethren, is how a brother is self-possessed. Then let a brother dwell mindful and self-possessed. This is my advice to you, brethren.

From the Pali Canon

Yet we all need relaxation, and what should be recreation. Even the most unruly dog must be let off the lead at times. Here are some hints.

CONCENTRATION AND RELAXATION

The wise man learns to walk before he runs; the wise man learns to concentrate before he meditates. But only practice makes perfection, and one must practise every day. Fortunately, one can practise concentration each moment of the day by applying the maxim—What thy hand findeth to do, do it with all thy might. But no engine will stand being run without intervals of rest, and it is equally important to learn to relax, physically and mentally. Neither is easy. There is an art in relaxing the body while sitting at one's work, and it is still more difficult to switch off the engine of the mind completely when it is not being usefully used. It is a paradox that to learn not to think is harder than to learn to think. The resulting mental control, however, is a faculty which is worth years of trouble to acquire, and it is an essential in true development.

Learn to distinguish between acts which need deliberate attention and acts which can be relegated to mechanical action. One can, for example, consider a problem worthy of the mind while shaving or knitting or walking to the post. On the other hand, the conduct of business or personal affairs of importance calls for complete concentration on the task in hand. Aim at learning to think clearly, swiftly and accurately, for the result will be three times the normal output with the minimum of wasted effort. It is a commonplace that it is the busiest men who are always punctual, businesslike, and can always 'find time' for what they wish to do.

Everyone knows the difference between the walk of the man who is physically fit and the slouching gait of the man who is flabby and slack in his physical condition. The same difference appears between the mentally fit and the mentally unfit. Deal with the matter in hand, crisply, firmly and at once, and then have done with it. Face each problem as a testing of one's spiritual condition, learn its lesson, do what seems right in regard to it without thought of the consequences to yourself, and then pass on to the next. By such constant practice the mind will become a trained and efficient instrument in the service of one's ideals, and when it is applied to meditation on the deeper problems of life its power will be found to be that of a searchlight lighting up the darkness of *avidya*, instead of a vague, uncertain flicker of a rushlight in the hands of a child.

Santana

And so to Meditation. *Why* do I meditate? To gain what, for whom, to be used to what end?

WHY DO I MEDITATE?

Unless the dangers confronting those who meditate are recognized at the beginning and taken to heart, there is grave risk of aspirants retreating from the Path in shame or fear, or both. The question 'Why do I meditate?' should be answered frankly, and then the answer examined. How much 'I' is there in the answer? The real strength of 'I' is only seen when the motive is pure. The more sullied the motive, the greater the spell of 'I'.

Is it to quieten the mind? If so what mind, and why have you allowed it to get agitated? To strengthen the mind? To what end, to be used to whose benefit? Or to find the Self? That sounds splendid but what does it mean to you? We are back on motive but it cannot be too often or powerfully stressed. If there is one way up this ladder there are at least a hundred ways of falling off it, and every one of them is labelled 'self'!

WAYS AND MEANS AND POSTURE

As this is not a book on meditation little is here said on methods, times and posture. It is not even assumed that meditation implies sitting in any posture at all, or anywhere or at any particular time. This Course is written for the wage-earner, not the monk, for the West and not for the East. As it is aimed at turning the whole strength of the heart–mind to its own already-arrived divinity it is claimed that this can be done at a bus stop or in a train, and in all the hundred little periods of time during the day when the attention need not be focused on anything else.

'To restrict oneself to the squatting posture all the time', said the Patriarch, 'is an infirmity, and unprofitable.

Listen to my stanza:
   A living man sits and does not lie down (all the time),
   While a dead man lies down and sits not.
   To this physical body of ours
   Why should we impose the task of squatting?'
                            Sutra of The Sixth Patriarch

Nevertheless the beginner will do well to form habits of time and place for regular meditation for ten minutes or an hour, and in the same place if possible, whether on the bed before rising or in a church in the lunch-hour.

As to posture in these special periods it is well at least to keep the spine erect and the hands and feet in some way folded; this for what

14

science would probably call electro-magnetic reasons, and the East by other names for a very long time.

MEDITATION ON A THEME

And so to meditation on a chosen theme. Or should we? The Lama Trungpa is fierce about the matter, and we should read what this modern authority on Tibetan Buddhism has to say.

THE LIMITATIONS OF MERE CONCENTRATION

There has been developed, in India and Tibet, a so-called system of meditation which might be called 'concentration'. It is based on focusing the mind on a particular point so as to be better able to control the mind and concentrate. In such practice the student chooses an object to look at, think about or visualize, and then focuses his entire attention upon it. In so doing, he tends to develop by force a certain kind of mental calm. I call this kind of mental practice 'mental gymnastics' because it does not attempt to deal with the totality of any given life-situation. It is based entirely on this or that, subject and object, rather than transcending the dualistic view of life.

Chögyam Trungpa in *Cutting through Spiritual Materialism*

Does this derogate from the whole purpose of this Course? If so, abandon it. But the venerable Lama speaks of the deep practices of Tibetan Buddhism, and we may reach this stage one day. The same applies to the long periods of meditation practised in the monasteries and especially the Zen monasteries of Japan. Meanwhile, in a busy, noisy, competitive Western world, earning our living, where the intellect tends to swamp the call of the heart and to ignore the call of the Spirit, let us try to think to the end of thought, and then arouse and develop the intuition and with its help find and become the Self we are.

As a master of Zen warns us, all our practice is but a means to an end which we may one day seek no more.

In meditation you separate yourself from the circumference of your environment and realize the Buddha in yourself. There is no other Buddhism in the world. The Master is in *here*. You have to knock at the door and ask to meet the Master! The answer comes from the *inside*, not the outside. But to call you must make an effort, must knock at the door of your heart. When you meet Him give up the knocking. At midnight if you try to get into a monastery, banging on the door with your fist, no answer. Then with a stone—'bang, bang'—'Yes'. Then you throw away the stone. Concentration and meditation are stones to find the Master; there comes a time when you do not need them any more. The door of the temple is not the Master; do not mistake it. Many people think that concentration and meditation are Buddhism.

Sokei-an Sasaki

I AM

Be seated, thou, unfettered, free,
The heart's attention poised as third of three.
Now still the mind, nor claim the unceasing flow;
He holds the unbounded heavens in fee
Who learns the uttermost command, let go.
Now seal with cold resolve the doors of sense.
Be still, my son, and seek thine immanence.

I am not body. I am never ill,
Nor restless, weary, fretful nor in pain.
I am not hot emotion, nor the will
Which forfeits progress in the name of gain.
I am not thought, the process of the mind
On caging partial truth intent,
Unknowing, for its eyes are blind,
The wings of life beat ever unconfined.
I am not any instrument.

I am the light that slays the night at dawning.
I am the love that woos its own reward.

I am the slow resolve that wakes at morning
And sleeps at twilight on a sheathéd sword.
I am the golden joy of beauty.
I am the stillness underlying sound.
I am the voice of undistinguished duty.
I am the Self in which the self is drowned.

T. C. H.

Am I—yet? Or is this but my 'self' very pleased with itself? We must all answer that one!

MEDITATION IN ACTIVITY

The Taoist classic *Saikondan* says, 'The stillness in stillness is not the real stillness; only where there is stillness in movement can the spiritual rhythm appear which pervades heaven and earth'. An ancient adds, 'Meditation in activity is a thousand million times superior to meditation in repose'.

From A First Zen Reader. Trevor Leggett

MEDITATE ALWAYS

Do not meditate only hidden in a dark corner,
  But meditate always, standing, sitting, moving, resting.
When your meditation continues throughout waking and sleeping,
  Wherever you are is heaven itself.

From Hakuin's Song of Meditation

QUESTIONS

1 Do you appreciate the distinction between Concentration and Meditation, the creator of the instrument and its use?

2 Can you concentrate on a chosen thing for minutes on end?

3 If not, on a process, such as music, or writing a letter or just breath, in spite of distractions outside and intruding thoughts within?

4 Can you concentrate on a thing or process while keeping out emotions and feelings of like and dislike, or fear?

5 How near is your power of concentration and control of thought to the modern searchlight?

SOME SUGGESTIONS ON THE USE OF THE COURSE

1 Read it. Then decide if you wish to take it as such. If you take it, give it a year's hard work, and 'don't wobble' as the Zen master said.

2 Decide clearly why, how and when you will use it, and consciously form the new habits needed.

3 Face its difficulty. There is here a new use of the mind and heart and emotions, the absorption and use of new ideas, the development of a new faculty.

4 Realize that if you start you must go quietly on. Don't rush it or overdo it, for there must be a reaction at a certain point, when you will be tempted to give it up.

5 Be ready to change your sense of values. The Course will create a new purpose in your whole life, including your religious exercises, if any, your worldly progress and your leisure, as well as your interrelation with all other human beings. Sooner or later you will have to decide which is to have priority.

Theme 1
BEYOND

Surely there *must* be a *Beyond* of phenomena, the things we know by our senses? Can we really conceive of a universe coming into being, developing and eternally changing which has no meaning or discoverable end? If there is such meaning where can it be save in life itself? But each of us lives in a complex form, at some stage of development, of life, and can there be two lives? Is not the life in every form one Life-force which is the universal force, the bursting life of the total cosmos, of all that is? If so, then the meaning and purpose of what we may call Life must exist in every form of it, including each of ourselves; in other words be already in the mind.

This is not a new suggestion, for it is implicit in theories and discoveries about the origin of the universe itself. And these are many, although again the manifold forms of it can be resolved into different or not so different versions of the same story. The first chapter of Genesis, studied as racial mythology and symbolic cosmogenesis, is clear enough. In the lovely simile of the Hindus, Brahman, the Absolute, 'breathed out' the universe, and after an almost inconceivable yet, so they claim, measurable period of time, 'breathed in' again. There are scores of stories of the Creation or Unfolding or Coming-to-be of the universe, and modern astronomers are adding more. But whether we accept their 'big bang' theory or the 'steady state' theory the universe has come from *something*, or may we not say Something, into its present complex condition.

But if we cannot as yet *know* the Absolute we can read and digest the greatest words about it, and thus slowly lift consciousness towards actual experience.

We can begin with Sir Edwin Arnold's verse translation of a famous passage from the Bhagavad Gita:

SPIRIT

Never the Spirit was born; the spirit shall cease to be never;
Never was time it was not; End and Beginning are dreams!

Birthless and deathless and changeless remaineth the spirit for
ever;
Death hath not touched it at all, dead though the house of it
seems!

Here are three more great passages.

THE ONE PRINCIPLE OF LIFE

It is only when all outward appearances are gone that there is left
the one principle of life which exists independently of all external
phenomena. It is the fire that burns in the eternal light, when the
fuel is expended and the flame is extinguished; for that fire is
neither in the flame nor in the fuel, nor yet inside either of the two,
but above, beneath and everywhere.

From the Mahaparinirvana Sutra.
Trs. the Master K.H. in *The Mahatma Letters to A. P. Sinnett*

The Secret Doctrine affirms:

An Omnipresent, Eternal, Boundless and Immutable
PRINCIPLE on which all speculation is impossible, since it
transcends the power of human conception, and could only be
dwarfed by any human expression or similitude. It is beyond the
range and reach of thought. . . .

From *The Secret Doctrine* of H. P. Blavatsky

The Buddha said:

There is, O Bhikkhus, an Unborn, Unoriginated, Uncreated,
Unformed. Were there not this Unborn, Unoriginated, Uncreated,
Unformed, there would be no escape from the world of the born,
the originated, the created, the formed.

The Udana

And this 'Unborn' is already within the utmost atom of the universe.

Truth is within ourselves; it takes no rise
From outward things, whate'er you may believe.
There is an inmost centre in us all,
Where truth abides in fulness; and around
Wall upon wall the gross flesh hems us in.

　　　　　. . . 'To *know*'
Rather consists in opening out a way
Whence the imprisoned splendour may escape,
Than in effecting entry for a light
Supposed to be without.

From Browning's Paracelsus

LOOK INWARD

Avert thy face from world deceptions; mistrust thy senses, they are false. But within thy body, the shrine of thy sensations, seek in the impersonal for the 'Eternal Man' and having sought him out, look inward; thou art Buddha.

The Voice of the Silence

Surely it must be so, whatever we call the Absolute, whether Almighty God or Parabrahman or the Buddha-mind or any other of the 'hundred names of God' which the Muslims describe. IT must be everywhere, in every form, large or small, including the form of every man or woman. Why, then do we look for it outside? What shall we find in the words of would-be Saviours, Swamis, Mahatmas, or even in the words of the greatest of these whom all regard as the great Teachers of mankind, or in a book, more than what the Zen people call 'a finger pointing to the moon'?

But the moon is within, and every finger points there. Surely at the most the great ones of our spiritual history can only teach us what to look for and where, whether in thought or in the meditation hour, or within the daily round.

For many of us this Nameless Beyond is first felt as Edwin Arnold described it in *The Light of Asia*.

Before beginning, and without an end,
　　As space eternal and as surety sure,
Is fixed a power divine which moves to good,
　　Only its laws endure.

Only *its* laws endure whether we call them the Laws of God or the Laws of Nature.

So it is 'all in the mind' or rather the Mind of the universe. This is an easy phrase to use, less easy to understand. For this Mind, call it as we will, is indeed God's Mind, Universal Mind, the Buddha-Mind, and it is all there, and always has been and always will be.

This tremendous truth is the whole theme of this Course, and it must at an early stage be thoroughly digested. A few more quotations may assist.

From the Lankavatara Sutra, one of the most famous of the whole Buddhist Canon:

Mahamati, to see all things as they really and truly are means to realize that there is nothing to be seen but Mind itself.

From the Zen Master Huang Po, one of the greatest Masters in all China and Japan:

All the Buddhas and all sentient beings are nothing but the One Mind, beside which nothing exists.

From Meister Eckhart, perhaps the greatest mystic produced in the West:

All things have been created out of nothing; therefore is the Nothing their true origin.

From the famous modern astronomer, Eddington:

Mind is the first and most direct thing in our experience. All the rest is remote inference.

Do these differ in their discoveries?

But many of our hearts are so full of self that little room remains for the Universe and THAT from which it came. We must empty our selves of all that makes for separateness.

TURN THE HEART ROUND

An Old Master said: 'Turn your heart round and enter the origin. Do not search for what has sprung out of it! When you have gained the origin, what has sprung out of it will come to you of itself. If you want to know the origin, penetrate your own original heart. This heart is the source of all beings in the world and outside the world. When the heart stirs various things arise. But when the heart becomes empty, the various things also become empty. If your heart is driven round by neither good nor bad, then all things are just as they are.

From *The Wisdom of the Zen Masters*. Irmgard Schloegl

These principles imply two levels of truth, the 'Namelessness', or THAT, as the Hindus call it, and 'This' which we know. We cannot discuss THAT, or ZEN or TAO, but we can and must study, and discuss, and apply our understanding of the process of each man's En-light-en-ment. For we are indeed already enlightened, as we are slowly discovering, having in us, as there is in every form of Life, a spark of the Unborn, the Buddha-Mind. So the process of enlightenment is a way of return, of becoming consciously more and more what we already ARE.

But the manifested universe is in size and duration far beyond the comprehension of our human minds. As for space, we now read of 'light-years' as units of space-time and of millions of light years between actually visible units of the now existing cosmos. As for time itself, it is now described by science in terms of almost unpronounceable length. Here is a delicious Indian story of the length of an aeon, in the East but a unit of time.

THE LENGTH OF AN AEON

Just as if, brother, there were a mighty mountain crag, four leagues in length, breadth and height, one solid mass of rock, and a man should come at the end of every century, and with cloth of Benares [the finest silk] should once on each occasion stroke that rock; sooner, brother, would that crag be worn away by this method, than the aeon.

From the Pali Canon

Surely this helps to stretch the mind to a better understanding of the sheer size of the present, visible universe, and therefore to move nearer to the concept, for such it is at the moment, of an Absolute Beyond?

But now contract the mind as far and as fiercely as this previous thinking has expanded it. We know how science has split the atom,

23

and the ever diminishing 'entities' within it; but consider this view of time.

This thing we are looking for, the Self as a spark of the Beyond, does not lie in the future, or in the past, or somewhere else. For, if we think it over quietly, there is no future. There is only now, and everything is here because we are always here. And all we can do at any time and in any place is this, what we are doing now. Tomorrow it will still be 'now', after a journey we shall still be 'here', and we never do anything but this thing, which we are doing here and now.

So our search is becoming easier. The meaning of life and hence its purpose is within, here, now and doing this; not in a vague future when we win a nice new job or the pools; not in some other place, in a new home or a meditation centre. Not doing something else, more splendid with apparently a better reward. In other words, we carry our problem *and its solution* in our present circumstances, as we are, here, now. And in the deeps of that complex, ever-changing thing called character or soul or the inner mind, or the Self.

But enough of peering at the mountain top through field glasses. Let us look more closely at that which has to climb.

IN SEARCH OF NOTHING

> Why look for it? Why seek it? Why demand
> Of each unravelled semblance this one thing
> Which none has seen nor yet can understand?
> We crave possession, comfortless; we cling
> To blind enquiry, hope that in some phrase
> Or virgin book or teacher's mouthing mind
> The hot hand of pursuit, in sudden blaze
> Of splendour, will magnificently find
> And hold it to the heart forever . . .
>
> > > > > > > Fools!
>
> It is, and is not found or bought or given.
> Effort, enquiry, search, these are the tools
> Of revelation. Not in earth or heaven
> Shall self, my self, ravish the final veil
> And, kneeling, see the face which has no face
> To see with, nor self-purpose to prevail.

Yet in that moment when the hands of space
Close to the compass of a point, not here
Not there, and time sleeps uninvented . . .
                                                    So,
The senses shall not find it anywhere.
'It lies within'. Oh clouded saying, No!
What of the host without if this within
Is the sole and royal servant of the Light?
Is earth we know a darkened wheel of sin,
And heaven alone the dim-illumined height?

It lives and moves. It changes not. It is,
Within without, to all men visible.
In laughter, love and in our vanities
    It is divided, indivisible.
It is beyond, and more. It has no being,
No hands of action, no disturbing will.
It sees and knows, yet no thing sees in seeing.
It is the whole of all yet each thing still.
It shines in no-self-ness, in right endeavour,
Fades when the one is falsely rent in two.
It waits, a moment stretched into forever,
Far, far beyond the reach of me or you.
Why seek it, then, in market place or mind?
Let it be lived and loved and deep enjoyed;
It is, we are, with nothing left behind.
How rich it is, that owns and is the Void!

From *Buddhist Poems*. Christmas Humphreys

QUESTIONS

1 Can you see that there must be a Beyond, beyond our thinking,
feeling and present utmost knowing, which is far beyond our
naming or description or the least thought of any form?

2 Can you conceive, which means to form a thought, at one stage
lower than this, but still immensely high in thinking, of all

25

existence, manifestation, unceasing becoming as one inseverable Oneness, the ONE, which is the Beyond now manifest to our senses, whether we understand the how and why or not?

3 If so, do you accept, at least as a mighty thought, that this Unborn Beyond or Absolute exists not only in this total Oneness but in every smallest particle of it? More poetically, that there is a Spark of the Light or Flame of Spirit in every form, visible and invisible, large or small, in every living thing, 'living' because there can be no thing dead?

4 Can you see that one of the 'things' in which this Flame is burning is you, and that others are your neighbours, friends and enemies? That each is *a* form of the same Almighty *You*?

Theme 2
SELF AND NOT-SO SELF

Self is the most complex and yet the most important 'thing' we know. It may be described as the ultimate goal of all spiritual search. 'Find the Self', say the sages, and all else follows. So let us look at ourself, our Self, forgetting for the moment its manifold divisions offered by theology, philosophy, psychology and, nowadays, science, and concentrate for the moment on our own experience of our own selves.

There is most obviously, a physical body. But we all speak of having a body, so here already are two parts of the self. This body is an animal, with a long evolution behind it. It has its reasonable needs and instincts, which we, whoever 'we' are, have to control. It needs food and warmth and shelter, a mate, and an agreed relation with the herd.

But what are we that order it about, earn food and warmth and shelter for it, and are concerned with its mating and the care of its young?

Let us leave this unanswered for the moment, and move from the bottom to the top of the scale. We are assuming that the Beyond is everywhere and in particular within. Let us call this ray of the absolute Light, this Life within every form, Spirit. It is not yours and it is not mine, and we cannot for the time being know it. But it IS. Now let us turn to St Paul's most helpful analysis of body, soul and spirit. Body we know, and a collection of faculties, or bases of consciousness, like the wavelengths on the radio, of which we are beginning to learn a little. We know of E.S.P., some of the faculties of the psychic plane which lies above the physical, and we all know of a desire centre which all too easily dominates our lives, a compound of over developed animal instincts and the cultivated capacity to derive pleasure from their exercise.

And Spirit we now know as a name for our highest faculty, even though it is never ours alone. It is like the light at the top of a lighthouse, a ray of sunlight shining in each self. It is the same in all.

But what lies between the two? What is soul?

You and I are more than our bodies but not yet one with Spirit. But we know 'soul' very well. We know of it, first, that it is not immortal, for it is clearly changing all the time, and rapidly. We can see, secondly, that it is immensely complex, an aggregate, a collection, some call it a mess, of qualities good and bad, of abilities and deficiencies, principles, convictions, beliefs; of loves and hates, hopes and fears, motives, ambitions and ideals. To which we may add a hotbed of desires, worthy and unworthy, circling round the ego, which is the false idea that I am different from you in essence and have rights and claims for myself alone. This 'soul' is thus a cauldron of fusing and dissolving ingredients, each moving up to the better and down to the worse on a spiral on which the whole is, so we hope, slowly rising towards Spirit and out of the clutches of the purely animal.

All this is included in what we call character or the individual. St Paul called it the soul. We have then the body, soul and spirit. But the soul is clearly at least dual. There is our daily mind, functioning, according to type, more as thought or feeling but together a thought-machine into which some programmer feeds the material which reappears as a business deal, an argument or a shopping list. But for many there is a level of mind above this, one which is capable of abstract thought, of large-scale understanding, of visions of great cosmic principles, of the deeper truths of life wherever expressed, whether in philosophy or religion, science or psychology, music or plans for the commonwealth. By virtue of this expansion of understanding we speak of many of our fellow men as having great minds, and the word great is well chosen.

But this 'body, soul and spirit' is not complete. Between Spirit which just IS and the individual mind, with even the finest intellect, there must be, and there is, some faculty, albeit poorly developed in most of us as yet, which is, as it were, a receiving set through which the absolute Light is caught and passed down into the mind, even as radio waves passing through a room need an instrument to make them audible. This faculty is the intuition, which alone *knows* Truth or any truth *directly*. For the intellect only knows more and more *about* any subject; it never *knows*. The distinction is clear and important for it marks the boundaries of the lesser faculties of thought, as in psychology or science. These experts know profoundly, but direct knowledge is a matter of personal experience. It is subjective. It comes and goes beyond our ordering. Its appearance may be a flash or a blazing light, and the greatest minds admit that in their efforts to know they are visited by these flashes which are the source of great discoveries, which the intellect then works out in the field of duality. And the force behind all these faculties, or high or low, is the will, and 'behind will stands desire'. Here is the complex field of motive and the right and wrong use of our powers.

But all these levels and principles and faculties are aspects of one inseverable Whole.

LEVELS OF EXPERIENCE

> Reality is One. The levels are not so many drawers in a chest, or even so many skins of an onion; they are levels of experience, and each level is an experience of the whole but in a given manner or with a given emphasis of attention.
>
> Sri Krishna Prem in *Man, the Measure of all Things*

Or, as another writer puts it:

> There is a connecting link which binds together the different levels of human experience, and there is a sense of hierarchy which maintains a proper order between these levels. There is no question here of the 'lower' being sublimated into the 'higher', but all the elements of our make-up are required to conform, each in its own terms, to the order of the whole, and to reflect, each upon its own level, the realities of which all life is, as it were, a revelation.
>
> Gai Eaton in *The Richest Vein*

These 'levels' should be under control, in the sense that at any time we should be conscious of the level on which this consciousness is functioning. Negatively, for example, we should be able to prevent emotion of any kind clouding our reasoning, or a toothache from making us lose our temper. Positively, we should in a sudden crisis see where the situation calls for cool, efficient action, as a doctor running to a man run over, or the expression of perfectly legitimate emotion in helping in another's grief.

Meanwhile we must learn to face the basic duality of our internal life, between mind and circumstance, between subject and object, between the Higher Self as we may call it and the lower self as it undoubtedly is.

SELF AND SELF

Rouse thou the self by self, by self examine self:
Thus guarded by the self, and with thy mind
Intent and watchful, thus, O mendicant,
    Thou shalt live happily.

Yea! Self is guard of self and refuge takes in self.
Just as a dealer trains a thoroughbred,
A noble steed, and breaks him to the rein,
    So do thou self restrain.

Dhammapada

'TO THINE OWN SELF BE TRUE'

This above all: to thine own self be true
And it must follow, as the night the day,
Thou canst not then be false to any man.
    From *Hamlet*. William Shakespeare

The tension produced by this basic duality is fierce in all of us, whether we call it between 'higher' and 'lower', or self and others, the calls of duty and the call for compassionate help for the suffering of others around one. We must admit it and learn to cope with it, for it explains much to ourselves and others of our own behaviour.

Note how we have, adding Theme number One to what is here said, already arrived at the famous trinity of St Paul, Spirit, Soul and Body. Spirit is a flame of THAT, the Unborn. Body is the personality, the man we know as we meet and work with him. The soul is the complex combination of factors in between, thought and feeling, emotion and will, ambition, fear and of the sense of triumph and disaster in our own affairs—illumined by some ray, fleeting or permanent, of the Light which forever shines, seen or unseen, within.

In passing we must deal however briefly with the strangely worded doctrine of the Buddhists of Ceylon and Burma and Thailand, who belong to the Theravada school as it is called, which was the first to spread Buddhism in England. Too lightly they say what, to many, is sheer nonsense, that 'There is no self—or Self'. But of course there is, and the Buddha never taught the opposite. What *did* he say?

'NO SELF'

> Every form must be regarded thus, as it really is, by perfect insight:
> 'This is not mine; not this am I; herein is not the Self of me'.
>
> From the Pali Canon

In other words, there is in man no *separate Immortal* Soul. For, as explained in Theme One, there is only Totality in manifestation, and inseverable Oneness, and for my petty 'self' to imagine otherwise is not only folly but the folly which produced the 'desire' for self which the Buddha described as the cause of most of our endless and intolerable suffering.

In time we do arrive, in the long ascent of the inner man to his own divinity, at a point of 'self-consciousness', and the term needs explaining. The following may help to unravel the apparent paradox as to its meaning.

SELF-CONSCIOUSNESS

> *Self-consciousness*, which from the animal plane looking upward is the beginning of perfection, from the divine plane looking downward is the perfection of selfishness and the curse of separateness. It is the 'world of illusion' that man has created for himself. 'Maya is the perceptive faculty of every Ego which considers itself a Unit, separate from and independent of the One Infinite and Eternal "Be-ness".' The 'eternal pilgrim' must therefore mount higher, and flee from the plane of self-consciousness it has struggled so hard to reach.
>
> William Q. Judge

Egotism, therefore, is for a period in our evolution right, but later becomes the stumbling block in the way of all spiritual—'no separate self'—progress.

The egotism with which we affirm our separate existence is a necessary adjunct to the evolutionary outflow, and only becomes our enemy when we seek to progress beyond its limitations. Neither the body, nor the sense-powers, nor the thinking, feeling complex are in themselves necessarily ego-structures. Egotism is a particular mode of feeling by which all these aspects of personality are exploited for the preservation of separateness.

Sri Krishna Prem in *Man, the Measure of all Things*

In what may be called this vertical tension between Self and self, the whole process of liberation from suffering, of becoming aware of the Absolute within the relative, of the Whole within its littlest part, is a contest, a fight for control. It is strange that the greatest scripture of the Theravada school of Buddhism, the Dhammapada, could not be more forceful on the nature of this everlasting struggle.

Self is the lord of self; who else could be the lord? With self well subdued a man finds a lord such as few can find.

And again:

Though one man conquer a thousand times a thousand men in battle, he who conquers himself is the greatest warrior.

Just how the Self copes with the self, the nagging ego whose sole interest is its self-advancement, is a matter for each to decide. We can make friends with it, fight it or just drop it!

DROP IT!

An aged Brahman came to the Buddha bearing gifts in either hand, and eager to receive enlightenment. Said the Blessed One: 'Drop it'. The Brahman let fall one of his gifts. Again the order came: 'Drop it'. The Brahman let fall the other gift and remained empty-handed. 'Drop it', came the order yet again. The Brahman was for the moment at a loss, then smiled, for he had attained enlightenment.

But above both there should be growing flashes of awareness, or at least a growing feeling of 'the Essence of Mind', the 'real man', Buddha Mind, Spirit, which is not yours or mine but which in essence we ARE. Is the following too difficult? It is important, lest in looking to a Higher Self we fall into the illusion of some Immortal Soul within us which is ours specifically.

THE HIGHER MIND

Even the Higher Self is not a permanent and indestructible monad. It is the individualized modality of Universal Mind; it is not a thing but a condition of or in consciousness. Throughout the entire universe there is one and one only Light of consciousness, life and power, universally diffused in Divine Mind, individualized in the Higher Self, separated by identification with psychic modalities in the empirical self, manifesting as life in the tissues of animals and plants, and as energy in the structure in minerals.

From *Man, the Measure of ali Things*. Sri Krishna Prem

THOUGHTS ON SELF

The title of this course was carefully chosen. It is indeed if rightly used a search within. What are we searching for? The answer is, if any word suffices, the Self, and we have reached a preliminary understanding of what this may be. The search becomes the purpose of life, the subject of all meditation, the background state of mind to all activity. We are seeking not for a magnified 'I' but for a force which grows increasingly to the extent that 'I' is felt to be *not*. Habitual consciousness is slowly raised. The individual feels himself more and more to be 'master of his fate' and 'captain of his soul'. 'To thine own self be true' becomes increasingly sound advice from the pen of a writer who, whatever his true identity, was a man of profound spiritual insight. Each of us, walking alone yet consciously part of all life about us, more and more lives in the undivided trinity of St Paul, Spirit, soul and body, for the interrelation grows with advancing knowledge of each.

The self is a folly of the thinking mind,
A thing, thought-made,
And we are blind in our imagining.

The fool, raising a seeking head,
Perceives and yearns with red desire.
Hands follow, craving to acquire
And grasp, themselves already dead.
('Be humble and remain entire').
The self, extruding from the Whole,
With knives of separation damns the soul.

The self is nought, a puppet filled with fear;
A swimmer set to violate the stream;
A voice the wakened Self must learn to bear
Or wake the dreamer from his foolish dream.

The universe is total, whole of will,
Unblemished harmony, and we,
Essential through eternity are still
Unsevered parts of void Totality.

SELF is. The Self, awake yet torn,
Strives riven-hearted to let fall
The weight of difference. (The All
Is partless, absolute, Unborn).

O SELF, that self in Self would die,
That Self, of all distinction free
Might slay forever, joyously
The fond, offensive thought of I!

T. C. H.

Finally, here is a collect of Wise thoughts on Self. Study and use them for they may at any time be needed.

The study of Buddhism is the study of self. The study of self is the study of the realisation of the nothingness of the self.

The Zen Master Morinaga

IT HAS BEEN SAID

Forgoing self the universe grows 'I'.
The Light of Asia

The sun casts no shadow.

We look at animals in cages. But each of us is caged within an animal. Do we look at ourselves?

None so empty as those who are full of themselves.

Self-gratulation, O Lanoo, is like unto a lofty tower up which a haughty fool has climbed. Thereon he sits in prideful solitude, and unperceived by any but himself.
The Voice of the Silence

It is well to bow at times. It matters not to what or whom so that the object is seen as something greater than oneself.

Man's first duty is to work out his own salvation from himself.
I. B. Horner

As one grows more one grows less.

All serve self, but our place in evolution may be judged by the size of the self we serve.

Enter into every man's Inner Self and let every other man enter into thine.
Marcus Aurelius

NO SELF, NO NOT-SELF

In the world of Reality
There is no Self, no other than Self
From the Zen poem 'On Trust in the Heart'

QUESTIONS

1 Who are you? He who knows the answer to this question is beyond this or any other similar Course! But we must seek the answer.

2 Who, then, are you, and who knows it? How many people, for example, would give a thought to you in six months' time if you were run over tomorrow? Does this question and the estimated answer trouble you? Which you?

3 Is the You in control of you as the driver of a car controls his vehicle. Do you love your car?

Theme 3
THE MIND AND ITS LIVING CONCEPTS

Of all the faculties of Self the most powerful it would seem is Mind, perhaps the finest instrument and the worst enemy of man's attempt to find the Self. Emerson was right.

Great men are they who see that spiritual is stronger than any material force; that thoughts rule the world.

Emerson

But man chooses the thoughts, for good or evil. This supreme power of creation, in science or metaphysics, philosophy or art, is at the same time the builder of concepts, thought-forms whether plans, conclusions, principles, choices, convictions, laws or empires which, with a thousand other forms, surround the Light within and tend to prevent the growing mind from perceiving it. Hence the rather frightening saying which comes early in *The Voice of the Silence*:

Mind is the great slayer of the real.
Let the disciple slay the slayer.

The solution to the paradox may lie in the level on which the thought is produced, although in a sense all thought, however splendid, is a fetter for those struggling to pass beyond the sway of thinking into that of *knowing* on the intuitive plane.

HIGHER THOUGHT

A person who is endowed with the faculty of thinking about even the most trifling things from the higher plane of thought has, by virtue of that gift, a plastic power of formation in his very imagination. Whatever he thinks about, his thought will be so far more intense that the thought of an ordinary person, that by this very intensity it obtains the powers of creation.

H. P. Blavatsky

37

This mind is unlimited. As Hui-neng, the famous sixth Patriarch of Zen Buddhism, announced:

THE ESSENCE OF MIND

Our Essence of Mind is intrinsically pure, and the reason why we are perturbed is because we allow ourselves to be carried away by the circumstances we are in.

And this is the true Creator of forms. The greatest saying of all the East is perhaps this: 'Waken the Mind to abide nowhere'. The revelation of the true meaning of this was enough to enlighten Hui-neng, as described in the famous Sutra of Hui-neng. When his master, alone with him in his room, came to the sentence, 'One should use one's mind in such a way that it will be free from any attachment', 'I at once became thoroughly enlightened, and realized that all things in the universe are the Essence of Mind itself'. And this is what lies within each one of us—already. 'You should know that as far as Buddha-nature is concerned there is no difference between an enlightened man and an ignorant one. What makes the difference is that one realizes it while the other is ignorant of it.'

But they can be closely aligned, and even become embarrassingly confused.

STRANGE DISCOVERY

I fret with trifles, uselessly discuss
Each truthless rumour of the world's affray;
Make furious plans of no importance, fuss
About the least disturbance of my day.
I want, appreciation. I demand,
Unfettered passage to my will, I grow,
To others' loss, and climb, until I stand
On pinnacles of self-engendered woe.
When Truth is enemy to self I lie;
Unless for profit why should I be kind? . . .

This horror bears two names; the first is I,
The second, less well-known, is Buddha-Mind.

T. C. H.

In the human mind is a vast array of its creations, some newly born and some decaying, cast away as the rubbish in a box-room. Memory, purpose, motive and imagination, ideals or sordid thinking, all that man has made and done is here, and the effects come home to roost, as we shall see more clearly when we come to Theme 7.

ANCIENT = MODERN THOUGHTS ON MIND

Ancient:
All that we are is the result of what we have thought; it is founded on our thoughts, it is made up of our thoughts.

Dhammapada

Modern:
Mind no longer appears as an accidental intruder into the realm of matter; we are beginning to suspect that it is the creator and governor of matter.

Sir James Jeans

THE MIND

Mind is the master power that moulds and makes,
And man is mind, and evermore he takes
The tool of thought, and shaping what he wills
Brings forth a thousand joys, a thousand ills:—
He thinks in secret and it comes to pass:
Environment is but his looking-glass.

Author Unknown

And all this power for good or ill is in each human mind, not merely in the hands of some all powerful, extra-cosmic God.

ALL IS WITHIN OUR SKIN

My friend, in this very body, six feet in length, with its sense-impressions and its thoughts and ideas, I do declare are the world, and the origin of the world, and the ceasing of the world, and likewise the Way that leadeth to the ceasing thereof.

From the Pali Canon

And it does get terribly full!

Nan-in, a Japanese Zen master, received a university professor who came to enquire about Zen. Nan-in served tea. He poured his visitor's cup full, and then kept on pouring. The professor watched the overflow until he could no longer contain himself. 'It is overfull. No more will go in!' 'Like this cup,' Nan-in said, 'you are full of your own opinions and speculations. How can I show you Zen unless you first empty your cup?'

From *Zen Flesh, Zen Bones*. Paul Reps

Let us consider a thought.

It is a 'thing', conceived and created in the workshop of the mind. It has shape, as a storm when seen from a plane has a measurable shape. It has duration, depending on the initial strength with which it emerged from the mind, and the measure of its repetition. It has strength, again depending on the mind which made it and the amount of will-power or desire which was put into it. It may be newly conceived or form but a part of a regular daily pattern with a weak 'charge', to use the inevitable analogy of electricity. It can be a controlled and planned creation, as for a family holiday or a new business, or a mere shopping list; or mere reaction to outside stimulus. In any event the force within it will be either that of a controlled will, or an accepted desire, or an emotion erupting, as psychologists say, from the unconscious. Much will depend on the degree of development of the 'mind', whether the higher or lower aspect of it, and this will largely determine whether the thought is 'good' or 'bad'. Such epithets cannot be defined, but generally speaking any thought-act, the motive for which is the commonweal, is at least 'better' than that which is aimed at the further expansion of the personal ego at the expense of all that stands in the way of it.

The wise man, then, learns to examine his thoughts and to begin to control them. There are and always have been a large variety of schools for thinking as well as schools of thought, and the present increasing interest in meditation is a symptom of the public's growing awareness of the need to control this vast potential of human energy. And the need for such control is urgent indeed.

Science is itself impersonal, but how it is used depends on a man's or a committee's or a nation's thought. We can now with the greatest ease blow each other to pieces, and may yet, before the end of the twentieth century, do so. Much will depend on whether world thought, for there is now such a force, is turned to the demands of the lower mind, for conquest and self-aggrandisement, or to the higher mind, for means of releasing the light of intuition, the sense of total oneness. Thus only will men advance, or at least the noblest of them, to ways of spiritual achievement beyond the demands of physical comfort and convenience.

The need for control is all the greater when we realize that no thought is propelled into a vacuum, nor dies with its creation. Soon we shall consider the ultimate, and to most of us frightening, law of cause-effect, which the East calls *Karma*, by which we are utterly responsible for the effect of every thought and feeling on the utmost particle of the universe. Once we begin to understand this living Law we shall be far more careful what we think, and to what end.

We should distinguish what we know, or think we know from what we merely believe.

BELIEF

Belief implies ignorance. We believe when we do not know. Knowledge, in the sense of intuitive conviction, comes from within. Belief, with its element of doubt, is superimposed from an outside source which has to be accepted on 'authority', and self-reliance is at an end. As missionary effort has abundantly proved, it is as easy to change another's beliefs as it is impossible to deprive him of what he knows. So long as one remains in a state of believing it matters little what one believes. Does it matter to an aboriginal native whether he believes that sacrifice to a totem will bring fine weather, or that grovelling penance to an unseen God will bring 'remission of sins'? Both beliefs are far removed from *knowledge* such as the Four Noble Truths of Buddhism, which need no 'faith' but can be verified in the laboratory of life.

Belief is coloured by desire and emotion, and the believing type of mind will generally believe just what it wants to believe, and ignore the converse. Compare this with the attitude of facing facts, whether pleasant or unpleasant, and whatever may be the pleasant or unpleasant consequences.

Beliefs may be found to be untrue. Knowledge can only be found to be but relatively true. We cannot, of course, know everything, but in the absence of knowledge we need not fall back upon belief. There remains the commonsense and scientific practice of accepting a reasonable hypothesis until experience can prove it to be true. Asked 'What do you believe?' a Buddhist would answer, 'Nothing, but I *know* that this and this is true and I think, and will tell you why I think, that this is also true'.

A Buddhist is always examining and testing the material presented him by circumstance, and thereby gradually develops the faculty of intuition wherewith to discriminate between the false and true. Where, then, is there room for belief?

Upasaka

We must learn to control this production of thought, to empty the mind and refill it at choice, a task of enormous difficulty as we shall soon discover. But it must be done.

EMPTY THE MIND

Empty the mind of the laden sad illusion
That you and I, regardant each to each
Are other, separate, apart,
Blind to the love-lit splendour of the heart
That lights the grey dark of the world's confusion . . .

Now fill the voided realms of heart and mind
With all the host of heaven. Add the tears
Of men and healing laughter. Look, and find
No corner where the heart once bled
But now with joy and splendour tenanted.

T. C. H.

But if thought and feeling, and powerfully held emotion are really such powerful forces ('thought rules the world') let us face the fact that each one we produce is affecting all around us.

THOUGHT

Every thought of man upon being evolved passes into the inner

42

world, and becomes an active entity by associating itself, coalescing we might term it, with an elemental—that is to say, with one of the semi-intelligent forces of the kingdoms. It survives as an active intelligence—a creature of the mind's begetting—for a longer or shorter period proportionate with the original intensity of the cerebral action which generated it. Thus, a good thought is perpetuated as an active, beneficent power, an evil one as a maleficent demon. And so man is continually peopling his current in space with a world of his own, crowded with the offsprings of his fancies, desires, impulses and passions; a current which reacts upon any sensitive or nervous organization which comes in contact with it, in proportion to its dynamic intensity.

H. P. Blavatsky

Here is the danger of arrogance, and the West is immensely arrogant about the truth of views it happens to hold at the moment about anything under the sun. Science at its less than best, and psychology, medicine and sociology, are all pathetically arrogant in the views held at the moment. Let us learn to be humble, or a little more so, so that as self is allowed to die we rightly use our increasing nobility of thought and the faculties which lie beyond it.

HUMILITY

Perhaps the oldest and most powerful advice on the subject comes from the Tao Te Ching, the classic of Taoism, in which it appears as a quotation from something earlier than, say, 500 B.C. 'Be humble and you will remain entire.' The fascination is in the word remain. And *The Voice of the Silence* has a delicious contribution.

SELF-GRATULATION

Self-gratulation, O Disciple, is like unto a lofty tower, up which a haughty fool has climbed. Thereon he sits in prideful solitude and unperceived by any but himself.

And Irmgard Schloegl tells a charming story from a sermon of a modern Zen master in Japan.

Master Sesso said, 'Though descriptions can be given, what really matters cannot be rendered in words. In front of a Shinto shrine a believer may be seen to pull the straw rope that summons the divinity, then clap his hands three times to indicate that he has come to worship, and then with folded hands bow deeply in the Presence. All this can be described down to the last detail. The divinity cannot be seen anyway. But what happens in the heart of the sincere believer in the act of bowing, that is the blessing. And that is indescribable.

From *The Wisdom of the Zen Masters*. Irmgard Schloegl

And of Humility it has been said:

Real humility does not consist in thinking little of yourself but in not thinking of yourself.
To love universally is true humility.

And of Mind it has been said

The perfect man employs his mind as a mirror. It grasps nothing; it refuses nothing. It receives but does not keep. And thus he can triumph over matter without injury to himself.

Chuang Tzu

Peace is in the mind, not in the circumstance.

Thucydides

You are not what you think you are, but what you think, you are.

QUESTIONS

1 'It is all in the mind?' Can you see the enormous truth of this? Or, better still, the Truth? Has the rule any exceptions? How could there be exceptions to it if it is the rule? If all our minds are dim and small reflections of Buddha-Mind or Spirit or the universal Mind, what lies without, save the projections of this Mind? Clearly, then, we must be careful how we use these tiny engines in our bags of skin or bodies, these units as they seem to be of Totality!

2 If you are the thinking type, has it occurred to you that the feeling type may arrive at Truth quite as quickly as you by yours? And

vice versa. And are the so-called introverts and extroverts different animals, or human beings with a mind which functions in opposite ways, as negative and positive electricity?

3 If you really accept the principle that Life is One, can you face its almost frightening consequence that as we look around on things and people and situations and those involved in them, 'there are no others'?

ALL LIFE IS ONE

Once the mind is examined, and its confused condition fairly accepted, and some effort made to abandon a large percentage of its attached concepts, including convictions about almost everything, it will be more open to new ideas, great cosmic principles of ideas. Then the time will be ripe to plant a seed-thought of these dimensions and, giving it full attention, see what happens as it ripens and grows. It may be found that it has rooted and is growing fast, pushing out earlier thoughts of a 'lower level' and profoundly changing the total character. Here may be the time to suggest such a cosmic principle by way of an all-day Theme. Accept it, examine it, chew it over, and above all try applying it to your total attitude of mind and action in all the happenings of the day. The phrase is simple enough, but almost frightening in its bursting power.

LIFE IS ONE

Accept this as true—utterly true, and work on it intensely with all its enormous implications and necessary change of habitual action, and see what has happened to your total self in three months' time.
An English poet knew it well.

... Feathered birds, and fishes finned,
And clouds and rain and calm and wind,
And sun and moon and stars, declare
All life is one life, everywhere;

That nothing dies to die for good
In clay or dust, in stone or wood,
But only rests awhile, to keep
Life's ancient covenant with sleep.

> From 'Elegy for Edward Thomas'.
> Charles Dalmon

LIFE AS AN INSEPARABLE WHOLE

As a philosophy, and also as a science of life, Buddhism is more comprehensive than any philosophical or scientific system yet developed in the Occident; for it embraces life in all its multitudinous manifestations throughout innumerable states of existence, from the lowest of sub-human creatures to beings far in evolutionary advance of man. In other words, Buddhism views life as an inseparable whole, beginningless and endless.

> W. Y. Evans-Wentz

Can one even conceive this to be untrue? Can one conceive a million things with each a different life informing iit? But if it is true, what follows? The answer needs a volume; but here are a few suggestions. You will find many to add as you really get down to applying the basic Theme.

1 NO SEPARATION

It is an occult law that no man can rise superior to his individual failings without lifting, be it ever so little, the whole body of which he is an integral part. In the same way, no one can sin, nor suffer the effect of sin, alone. In reality there is no such thing as 'separateness', and the nearest approach to that selfish state, which the laws of life permit, is in the intent or motive.

> H. P. Blavatsky in *The Key to Theosophy*

2 THERE IS NO DEATH

There is no death. There is only the unceasing cycle which the Buddhists call the Wheel of Life, of birth, growth, decay and death, applying to every thing, visible and invisible. All forms die as Life exhausts them, as the electric light bulb 'dies' when worn out and is replaced with a new one. The 'opposite' of death is birth, not life. All that is born will die—some time. Life flows on through all the opposites and remains entire, as a total manifestation of Totality, Spirit, Buddha-Mind. Forms are, but not as separate things.

Entities are real, but not in the sense of being truly separate from one another, of having each its own-being.

Aldous Huxley

3

All men are brothers. All forms of life, visible or invisible, are brothers. Can we learn to act accordingly, all day? The results are profound. Can we now hate—anyone, despise, be jealous, of anyone? He is you! Shall we not strive to understand him, be active to help him, recognize in him just one more ever-changing form of the one Totality, as another form of the same One Life? He is you! Jesus said we should love the Lord our God (Spirit, Buddha-Mind) and our neighbour, as ourself. Strong words indeed. Do we even strive to obey? Yet, as will be quoted again and again, in truth we needs must pay attention to the needs of others for 'There are no others . . .'.

IT HAS BEEN SAID

All forms are forms of life. But can there be more than one Life in these forms? If not, should we not behave to all beings as forms of the same One Life?

Look with an equal eye on all things, seeing the One Self in all.

Bhagavad Gita

Look to the Light and worship the Light, and judge not the forms through which it shines.

Thou shalt not separate thy being from Being, and the rest, but merge the Ocean in the drop, the drop within the Ocean.

The Voice of the Silence

(Compare this with the well-known last line of Edwin Arnold's *The*

Light of Asia, 'the Dewdrop slips into the shining Sea'. For some say that what happens is the other way round, or that this is what it feels like.)

QUESTIONS

1 Do you accept, as a powerful new idea, the fact that the life in every form without exception is the same one Life?

2 Can you accept, though perhaps less clearly, that such life is the one Life-Principle or Buddha-Mind or the Absolute which manifests as the universe?

3 If so, do you realize the enormous change which this must bring about in your mind? Of friendliness to every living thing; and tolerance of their difference; that the universe is a collective life-form and that within it 'there are no others'?

4

   'Hast thou attuned thy heart and mind to the great heart and mind of all mankind?'

The Voice of the Silence

Theme 4
SUFFERING AND ITS CAUSE, DESIRE

The Buddha pointed out that all things have three factors in common, and these Three Signs of Being are the basis of the teaching of the oldest school of Buddhism.

They are the omnipresence of change, applying to every thing, including all the parts of man, without exception; the fact that no thing whatsoever has a permanent, immortal and unchanging 'soul' or Self which is separate from the total Self of the universe; and that all things are suffering, inseparable from suffering.

The word translated here as suffering, in Pali *dukkha*, has many meanings, including physical pain, disease and the disabilities of such, and of old age, emotional fear, jealousy and sense of loss, mental doubt, confusion and remorse, and even a sense of frustration or inadequacy in one's ability to find out and thus know what alone is worth our knowing. All this and more was compressed into the Buddha's famous oft-repeated declaration,

One thing I teach, O Bhikkhus, suffering and the end of suffering.

The Buddha found the cause of suffering in the presence in all of us of the desire, craving, clinging inherent in the illusion of 'I', in the false belief that I am different from, separate from other forms of the one Life-force born of the Unborn Absolute. Here is 'the great dire heresy of separateness that weans thee from the rest' referred to in *The Voice of the Silence*, and he who sees this as the cause of suffering is becoming wise indeed.

The suffering itself does not purify; it is but evidence of a purifying process at work, as a rash upon the skin, but until the cause is worked out and removed the suffering will continue.

Meanwhile the relationship between the Three Signs is of deep importance. Do we really accept that all, literally every 'thing' is changing all the time, and all of it? Do we accept that this includes all of 'me', including the loud-mouthed 'I'? We should meditate on these facts, for facts they are, of unceasing change and non-permanentselfness, for together they cause much of the third Sign, Suffering.

We dislike suffering, but it is a great teacher, and some say the only teacher.

THE NEED TO SUFFER

Woe to those who live without suffering. Stagnation and death is the future of all that vegetate without change. And how can there be any change for the better without proportionate suffering during the proceeding change?

H. P. Blavatsky

Truly we are on the Cross. Tension of the Opposites pulls us both ways at once. At the same time tension of the Higher Self pulling up while the lower, false ego, at least holds us down in the mire produces a dual strain at the centre, which may fairly be described as the Cross which is at the heart of suffering, and he is truly dead to the world whose ears are deaf to the 'still, sad music of humanity'. We shall indeed know suffering until the ego is in some way brought under control.

All who descend into birth must suffer and cause suffering, must act and be acted on, must learn and be the instruments of learning. For our task is to learn through experience, to learn how to handle, to harmonize, and in the end to master the elements of experience, until finally the compulsive self-identification with the form is broken, and we come to know ourselves in the freedom of our true nature.

From *Man, the Measure of all Things*. Sri Krishna Prem

Meanwhile, there are many ways of dealing with the cold fact of suffering.

SUFFERING

To suffer it to suffer well, to accept
The untoward circumstance, to bear with skill
The weighted balance which the fool, inept
In equilibrium, would strive to kill
With flight or malediction. Would he thrust
With hand of will the pendulum of rule

From powered harmony? The law is just
And swings upon the wise man as the fool.
To receive, to suffer wholly, to digest
The living deed's implicit consequence,
Here's error's absolution; full confessed.
The deed dies in the arms of immanence.
To suffer is to grow, to understand.
The void of darkness holds a proffered hand.

T. C. H.

And this 'hand held out' is knowledge of the cause of it, the object and supreme triumph of the Buddha's age-long search. He put the result of his discovery in four immortal propositions. There is suffering; its cause is desire; if we remove the cause we remove the effect, and the Way to remove the cause will be found in the Noble Eightfold Path. This Path is itself an age-long Course in the finding of the Self, which lies beyond self and its unceasing folly. But desire itself is neither good nor evil, but the driving force behind the will. It operates on all 'levels' of the total Self. At low level it is self-ish unworthy low desire the training to abstain from which is the third Precept of the Theravada School. At its highest level it merges into Compassion, a desire to serve and save all beings.

As *Kama* it receives firm handling in *The Voice of the Silence*, a Tibetan scripture which may well be pre-Buddhist.

Kill out desire; but if thou killest it, take heed lest from the dead it should again arise.

Strive with thy thoughts unclean before they overpower thee. Use them as they will thee, for if thou sparest them and they take root and grow, know well these thoughts will overpower and kill thee. Beware, Disciple, suffer not, even though it be their shadow, to approach. For it will grow, increase in size and power, and then this thing of darkness will absorb thy being before thou hast well realized the black foul monster's presence.

Do not believe that lust can ever be killed out if gratified or satiated, for this is an abomination inspired by Mara. It is by feeding vice that it expands and waxes strong, like to the worm that fattens on the blossom's heart.

But this is self-ish desire, the animal's lusts not yet controlled. And behind will stands desire. What is the difference? Surely will is the motive force, call it what you will, of all action on any plane, the Life-force of the universe in manifestation. It is the powerful vehicle or car. But the driver is here desire, who can drive the car where he will. Hence the need to 'divinize' desire, to raise it to impersonal, self-less level or at least nearer to it, until desire itself, no longer evil, merges in pure compassion.

Here again is the high and the low, the Self and the self, in conflict, until in some way merged in unity.

Desire nothing. Chafe not at Karma nor at Nature's changeless laws. But struggle only with the personal, the transitory, the evanescent and the perishable.

The Voice of the Silence

WILL AND DESIRE

Desire, in its widest application, is the one creative force in the Universe. In this sense it is indistinguishable from Will; but we men never know desire under this form while we remain only men. Therefore Will and Desire are here considered as opposed.

Thus Will is the offspring of the Divine, the God in man; Desire the motive power of the animal life.

Most men live in and by desire, mistaking it for will. But he who would achieve must separate will from desire, and make his will the ruler; for desire is unstable and ever changing, while will is steady and constant.

Both will and desire are absolute *creators*, forming the man himself and his surroundings. But will creates intelligently—desire blindly and unconsciously. The man, therefore, makes himself in the image of his desires, unless he creates himself in the likeness of the Divine, through his will, the child of the light.

His task is twofold: to awaken the will, to strengthen it by use and conquest, to make it absolute ruler within his body; and, parallel with this, to purify desire.

Anonymous

What, then, can we do about suffering save look to its cause and see that the cause be not repeated? We shall learn more of causation at cosmic and human level when we examine the Law of Karma in Theme 7. For the moment it is enough to point out the obvious, that we must accept the results of past wrong causes, raise the level of our present habitual desiring, and so reduce our own suffering and enable us the better to reduce in some minute degree 'that mighty sea of sorrow formed of the tears of men'.

THE END OF SUFFERING

Clearly there must be many ways of ending the causes of suffering. Somehow we must raise, sublimate, transform the lower self here called ego, the false I, to live more in the Self of which it is the unworthy adjunct.

Clearly we begin by recognizing its existence and ceasing to blame anyone or anything else for its cause.

We can see that its cause is self-ish desire and then slowly change our habitual attitude to every sort of trouble that besets us.

Here is another suggestion

DESIRE

I cried aloud to God, that stood in fire.
But God, it seemed, had heard of my desire
Before,
And, as he played upon the floor
His children all about him, said,
Nor raised his head,
'Well, why not drop it?'

T. C. H.

BETTER STILL?

The best remedy for evil is not the suppression but the elimination of desire, and this can best be accomplished by keeping the mind constantly steeped in things divine.

H. P. Blavatsky

But how do we eliminate wrong or low desire? The answer is easy to give but hard to apply—by removing the cause of low desire, the ego or untrue self.

This, of course, is the result of our own past wrong thinking, feeling and desiring, and we must begin to substitute right—unselfish, for wrong—selfish desire. For, as Dr Suzuki says, 'the ego in this sense is but the will in a state of ignorance'.

We can usefully work at a new distinction, that between pleasure-pain and happiness. Make the effort to be less interested in both pleasure and pain. Neither produces or prevents the presence of happiness. But happiness itself is a false and selfish notion. How can we be happy, whatever we mean by that term, when the man next door is dying of cancer, and the woman on the other side has just lost her baby? Is there nothing higher which will help to raise the level of our own desire? Yes, if we take the trouble to study the factors involved. What is our real purpose in life now? To do what? And why do we want to do it? Is the double factor of purpose/motive rising in quality day by day? If so, the result can be permanent indestructible Joy—beyond pleasure/pain, beyond happiness, beyond all suffering.

This Joy is on the level or wave-length of the Self, our 'flame of the Buddha Mind'. Sorrow will always be with us, for Life is one and all sorrow is ours, as all happiness if we want it, and all Joy which none can take away. We shall still have toothache, and illness and troubles of all kinds, but somehow the habitual level of mind will be rising steadily and these things will matter less and therefore be more easily bearable.

THE EGO

Only the ego can be frightened, only the ego can lose property, be insulted, be hurt, feel pain. The ego, being a flimsy construction and being bound up in time and space, will have to fall apart. The ego, in fact continuously falls apart and has to be reinforced by vanity, greed, jealousy and evil.

From *A Glimpse of Nothingness*. De Wetering.

Here, then, is a new perspective, a new set of comparative values.

I SEE A STAR

I see a star. It is not there. It is not there for a million light-years, a term which has no meaning for my mind. Light travels, I am told, at so many miles a second. I multiply by sixty and by sixty to make this miles an hour. I multiply by the days of the year and then by a million, reaching a figure followed by twelve noughts. This is a concept, thought or symbol which has no meaning for my mind. So far away in space and time there died that star which, here today, I see.

On earth I have three thousand million friends. Each, born of the same Unborn, a form of the same one Life, has appetites like mine. Each wills to grow in order that self, its own especial fantasy, may steadily expand though others die.

I see no sense in this; it breeds but pain. I shall arise and gather in the flock of my desire, remembering my unimportance, seeing, with opened eyes, that star.

From the meditations of Komo Ki

The ideal, then, seems obvious. We must face suffering and its cause, self-ish desire, and then rise to reduce the cause until the only will left is merged in a desire to co-operate with the Plan as best we may.

IT HAS BEEN SAID

Much more has been said of Desire at all its levels. Here is a selection:

There are two ways of being disappointed; getting what you want and not getting it.

William Gerhardi

The truly happy are those who bring their desires in line with their duty.

Greater is the pain of those that are possessed by desire than the pain encountered on the way of holiness, and no Enlightenment comes to them.

Desire what you will but don't send your self to fetch it.

You cannot prevent the birds of sadness from flying over your head, but you may prevent them stopping to build their nests in your hair.

From the Chinese

Servitude to the desire for pleasure is the most intolerable of all forms of slavery to which mankind has subjected itself.

By concentrating the thoughts one can fly; by concentrating the desires one falls.

The Secret of the Golden Flower

Freedom is doing what you like, but freedom is Zen and Zen means liking what you do.

R. H. Blyth

If thou hadst known how to suffer, thou wouldst have been able not to suffer. Learn thou to suffer, and thou shalt be able not to suffer.

The Acts of St John

Everything is ours, provided that we regard nothing as our property. And not only is everything ours; it is also everybody else's.

Aldous Huxley

Want a thing long enough and you don't.

How shall I grasp it? Do not grasp it. That which remains when there is no more grasping is the Self.

The Panchadasi

And to conclude:

Life is sweet, brother. There's night and day, brother, both sweet

things; sun, moon and stars, brother, all sweet things; there's
likewise a wind on the heath.

George Borrow

QUESTIONS

1 Do you realize that desire is a force which functions on many
levels, differently at different periods of our existence and at
different periods of the day?

2 Do you agree that desire is 'good' or 'bad' according to the
development of the mind producing it, the occasion, purpose and
motive for the expression of it?

3 Do you see that desire, right for the animal, and the animal in us,
can cease to be right for the developed man? And that desire for
Nirvana may be the right desire/energy until the very last stages
on the road to it?

4 And can you see that, at the very highest level, desire merges into
universal compassion?

STRENGTH

Strong is the oak until time fells it.
Strong is the Void until thought fills it.
Strong is the sea, and the wind, and a raging fire.
But strongest is the strength of no desire!

T. C. H.

RIGHT ACTION, REACTION AND NON-ACTION

ALL IS ACTION

From the moment the 'Unborn' is born on to the field of manifestation, until this 'unrolling of the worlds', as it is called in the Pali Canon, becomes 'the rolling up of the worlds', *all is action*. Nothing *is* save a ceaseless process of 'coming to be, coming to be' followed by 'ceasing to be, ceasing to be'. Life is motion and all is alive. Forms are born, grow, grow old and wear out—Life goes on, Life, the creative/destructive force of manifestation whether known as Spirit, Buddha-Mind or Almighty God. Nirvana is awareness of the Void of separate forms; Samsara is the changing world of forms. Each is a mode of the other; 'Form is emptiness and the very emptiness is form', says the Heart Sutra. Wisdom *is* action. Thus although Samsara is one vast bubble of *maya*, illusion, we live and grow and attain enlightenment within this illusion, suffering its inevitable tension of duality and involved in its unceasing action, whether its form be action, reaction or no action.

In brief, we are all acting all the time, but we are here concerned with Right action in the world of men. This involves right relations with all other forms of the One Life. We have suggested that the threefold task of any man on the Way is Study, Digestion and Application. We have now reached Application, both without and within ourselves.

The importance of daily and indeed hourly application of the principles we have accepted provisionally as true cannot be overestimated. As pilgrims we are climbing the mountain all the time. We only learn by doing. Mahayana Buddhism stresses, as we shall see, the twin forces of Wisdom/Compassion, and the former is useless without the latter. Compassion is wisdom in action, and most action which is not the compassionate product of right awareness is worse than useless; it may be the father of evil action, causing untold suffering in days to come. But there must *be* action.

THE NECESSITY OF ACTION

'If a man talks much about the Teaching but does not live in accordance with it, he is a cowherd counting another's cattle. He is no disciple of the Blessed One. But if a man can recite but little of the Teaching, *yet puts its precepts into practice*, ridding himself of hatred, craving and delusion, cleaving to nothing in this or any other world, he is a disciple of the Blessed One.'

The words of the Dhammapada above italicized contain the essence of all religious teaching since the world began. Herein lies the distinction between the man of words and the man of action, the man who argues and the man who is.

Wisdom has been defined as spiritual knowledge applied to material things. Mere knowledge is accumulated in each life by the brain, but, like all other material belongings, it dies at death. Only so much of it as has been transmuted by experience into faculty will pass the barriers of death, and be of value in the lives to come. Let us, therefore, beware of acquiring knowledge for its own sake, lest, like the now familiar figure of the scientific specialist, we learn 'more and more about less and less,' and in the major crises of life find that all our learning is of no avail.

No scientist accepts a theory until he has tested it from every angle and found that it is true. How, then, are those of us who study and write about Buddhism entitled to do so until we have tested and experienced the doctrines which we teach? But the only testing ground for theory, the only laboratory of life is the world of everyday, the world of buses, tubes and factories, of office hours and monotonous routine. The inner life of true development does not begin when the hand of Karma first leads us to a life of meditative ease. It began ten thousand lives ago and is in progress now.

Between the world of theory and the world of practice lies a bridge across which each one of us must ultimately pass, but we shall not cross it until we begin to move. A car may be filled with the finest petrol, but it will not move forward until the engine is put in gear. While we theorize and discuss our power to progress remains potential, and only becomes dynamic when applied.

It has been said of belief that a man believes a thing when he behaves as if it were true. Do we behave as if the law of change were true, or do we try to possess things for ourselves and build up a barricade of them behind which to 'settle down'? Do we accept the need to meditate regularly and with the whole strength of the will? Do we realize that it is more blessed to give than to receive, and behave accordingly, and do we give from the heart or let the brain dictate what we can 'afford'? Do we ever remember that 'all we are is the result of what we have thought', and use our thought to build up character and circumstances for the days and lives to come, and do we above all realize the nature of self and the pitiful foolishness of personal desire? If not, all reading, lectures and meetings are waste of time. We are still looking at the Path and not treading it. As a Zen master said to an enquirer who asked the nature of the Path, 'Walk on'. Only so shall we cross the bridge which divides Samsara from Nirvana and find ourselves disciples of the Blessed One.

Santana

What, then, is an act? It is the expression of a thought or feeling, new or old, or of habit, or a form of reaction to a new situation. We cannot 'opt out' nor escape from the stream of life of which we are an undivided part.

Each act is charged with purpose and motive, however unnoticed each may be. There is a considerable difference. Purpose is what we are trying to do; motive is why we are trying to do it. Purpose needs no further explanation but we must pause to consider motive. We should know, and clearly, just what it is, whether the act be large or small, for the motive and the act are ideally one.

RIGHT MOTIVE

Says Krishna to his pupil Arjuna in the Bhagavad Gita:

Let, then, the motive for action be in the action itself, and not in the event. Do not be incited to actions by the hope of their reward, nor let thy life be spent in inaction. Firmly persisting in Yoga, perform thy duty, and laying aside all desire for any benefit to thyself from action, make the event equal to thee, whether it be success or failure.

One is reminded of the lines in Kipling's poem, 'If',

If you can meet with Triumph and Disaster,
And treat those two impostors just the same ...

Or, to return to the Gita, try practising the advice I use each day upon myself, 'A constant and unwavering steadiness of heart upon the arrival of every event, whether favourable or unfavourable'. Surely this is a better motive than the enlarging of the self! For surely it is true, 'the Way is to be sought for its own sake, not with regard to your feet that shall tread it'.

All this needs enormous effort. We are back on the battlefield of Self versus self, and the way of gentleness *may* bring about results. There is precedent for thinking something stronger is needed.

BUDDHIST WARRIORS

Warriors, warriors, Lord, we call ourselves. In what way are we warriors?
We wage war: therefore are we called warriors.
Wherefore, Lord, do we wage war?
For lofty virtue, for high endeavour, for sublime wisdom—for these things do we wage war. Therefore are we called warriors.

From the Pali Canon

What else throughout the day is half as important?

The man who wars against himself and wins the battle can do it only when he knows that in that war he is doing the one thing which is worth doing.

H. P. Blavatsky

Yet every machine needs rest. Work and play are one more of the pairs of Opposites, so long as 'rest' is not our synonym for laziness.

RELAXATION

In all the activities of life, from the most trivial to the most important, the secret of efficiency lies in an ability to combine two seemingly incompatible states—a state of maximum activity and a state of maximum relaxation.

Aldous Huxley

What action? There can be no answer to this from another, for none can dictate what another should rightly do. In matters spiritual he can, however, when asked for it, advise.

THE POWER DIVINE

Sir Edwin Arnold has a fascinating passage in his famous poem, *The Light of Asia*.

Pray not, the Darkness will not brighten,
Ask
Nought from the Silence for it cannot speak.

Then he leads up to the great verse following:

Before beginning, and without an end,
  As space eternal and as surety sure,
Is fixed a Power divine which moves to good,
  Only its laws endure.

This is profound teaching from the Buddhist scripture on which his poem is based. But it is imperative that we do not misunderstand the nature of this Power. It is not a Personal God, nor any Saviour, human or divine. Yet it calls for obedience, by the total man. By what right? Because this Power is All-Power, the voice of Spirit, the Voice of the Silence, the divine imperative within to do 'my Father's business', which is to work towards the total Plan of the total manifested Universe. This is right purpose and right motive combined—what to do and why. And a growing sense of obedience solves the irritating problem of good and evil, or right and wrong.

GOOD AND EVIL, RIGHT AND WRONG

A man does evil deeds by going on the wrong path through desire, through hatred, through delusion and through fear.

From the Pali Canon

Good and bad alike are relative states upraised on attachment to what is called self. Good is based on attachment to selfhood in a state which still leaves considerable track of impurity. And of course evil leaves a great track. Good is not good if it is all with the idea of getting something out of it. . . . It is a good but with oneself at the centre. All would be well if I made the heart empty and forgot the fact that I am doing a good action . . .

From the Master Obora. The Tiger's Cave. Trevor Leggett

We must here watch that we keep a delicate balance. Once compassion is roused in the heart we want to help all forms of suffering everywhere. But it is all too easy to interfere in others' affairs and imagine we are doing good. As the Bhagavad Gita insists, there is danger in another's duty. But the Voice of the Silence provides the opposite and equally important point of view. 'Inaction in a deed of mercy is an action in a deadly sin'. Intelligence must help us to decide, and there must be constant watchfulness on motive. At least refute the lazy selfish minds that sneer at all 'do-gooders' just because much social service is ill-advised and tactlessly applied.

HELP

(By an Unrepentant Do-gooder)

Our days are filled with action and reaction, part deliberate and part the reflex of our mind's conditioning.

In this we are concerned with fellow human beings, all of whom are changing every moment in all their parts, are suffering, and possess no principle which permanently separates them from other forms of life.

But Buddhism teaches that life is one, that what we call Samsara is a collective manifestation of the 'Unborn, Unoriginated Formless' which the Hindus just call THAT.

It follows that all human beings are sons of the same Father, and are therefore brothers.

It follows that we are deeply concerned with others' suffering, for indeed 'there are no others'. Our suffering is theirs and theirs is ours. We know too well 'that mighty sea of sorrow formed of the tears of men', and all contribute to it.

The cause of suffering, said the Buddha, is self-ish desire. Do all men realize it? If not, should we not help to make this discovery better known to all mankind? And daily, should we not help our brother, neighbour, friend or even enemy, if we are foolish enough to have one, with money, effort, thought and time, in crises large and small? If it is not easy to 'love thy neighbour as thyself' should we not try? Or look into our own minds to see why not?

'Cease to do evil. Learn to do good. Cleanse your own heart', says the Dhammapada. Note the order. And note that we have to learn how to do good. We need wisdom to guide our compassion as it wakens.

What is the result of this unceasing attitude of mind? First, it reduces self to a minimum and hence our suffering. Secondly, it reduces, so far as lies in our power, the suffering of our fellow men, and helps them to happiness, and thence to joy and thence just so much nearer to Enlightenment. The world would be a lovelier place were we all so occupied.

Why, then, this modern sneer by many at 'do-gooders'? Because in the past, and now, it is all too often tactlessly performed? Or because it does not lead directly to Enlightenment? Of course not in itself, but are we all so heavily concerned with our own enlightenment? In the Theravada we read of the ascending scale of love known as the four Brahma Viharas. In the Mahayana, the Bodhisattva is concerned with nothing else than the enlightenment of all men, indifferent to his own.

As a would-be Buddhist I seek no better epitaph than this; 'He went about doing good'.

Santana

GOOD AND EVIL

We say that good and evil *exist*, but to assert the *Being* of Good would imply the *Being* of Evil. Evil is negative and merely *ex-ists* in so far as Reality is seen from the point of view of diverse particularity.

Note from *The Diamond Sutra*, trs. A. F. Price

ACTION 'RIGHT' AND 'WRONG'

How shall we know the difference? What is good and what is evil? The answer lies in motive, which is not the same thing as purpose or intent. The purpose of meditating, for example, may be to gain mind-control. The motive for this may be the better to serve mankind, but it may also be to get the better of a business rival, or to put oneself forward as a great teacher. Indeed, 'there's nothing good or bad but thinking makes it so', and the test is the presence of self. Are we flowing *with* the cosmic tide in all we think and do, or against it? Are we working for self or for the whole? Moving inwards towards the centre or outwards towards difference, distinction and the self's aggrandisement?

It has been said that the perfect act has no result, for there is no one there to receive it. There was right action, indifferent to result. As Tennyson wrote in Oenone,

> Self-reverence, self-knowledge, self-control,
> These three alone lead life to sovereign power.
> Yet not for power (power of herself
> Would come uncalled for), but to live by law
> Acting the law we live by without fear;
> And because right is right, to follow right
> Were wisdom in the scorn of consequence.

And the law we live by is the Law of Karma, of cosmic harmony, of cause-effect in this life and all others, past and yet to come.

In brief,

> Do the work that's nearest
> Though it's dull at whiles,

66

Helping when you meet them
Lame dogs over stiles.

Charles Kingsley

So much for Action, but what of its opposite, Inaction? The entire religion, if it can be called a religion, of Taoism, founded, as was Buddhism, in the sixth century B.C. but in China, largely rests on the right understanding of 'Non-action'. It is all too easy, says the Taoist, to exhaust yourself and others in rushing about in ceaseless action. The man at rest within himself finds action acting, so to speak, without his intervention. This is no easy matter.

> The Secret of the magic of life consists in using action to achieve non-action. One must not leave out the steps between and penetrate directly.
>
> *The Secret of the Golden Flower*

There is a distinction between Non-action and inaction.

> Non-action prevents a man from becoming entangled in form and image. Action in inaction prevents a man from sinking into numbing emptiness and a dead nothingness.
>
> *The Secret of the Golden Flower*

CARL JUNG ON 'LETTING THINGS HAPPEN'

> Let things happen, for, as Master Lu Tzu teaches in our text, the Light circulates according to its own law, if one does not give up one's accustomed calling. The art of letting things happen, action in non-action, letting go of oneself, as taught by Master Eckhart, became a key to me by which I was able to open the door to the 'Way' . . .
>
> From his comment on *The Secret of the Golden Flower*

> Both action and inaction may find room in thee; thy body agitated, thy mind tranquil, thy Soul as limpid as a mountain lake.
>
> *The Voice of the Silence*

TWO KINDS OF INACTION

There are two kinds of inaction; the cessation of all mental and bodily effort, and the state wherein a man does not identify himself with his thoughts and his deeds. It is this second condition, this surrender of the personality, which is the highest form of inaction, and for this reason it has been called action in inaction. The self is composed of a number of qualities—form, feeling, perception, tendency, consciousness—and our being is the result of these qualities moving amongst each other, of the senses reacting to the objects of sense. When a man identifies himself with the movement of these qualities there is action; when he identifies himself with their coming to rest there is inaction, but in both cases he is the victim of egoism and self-deception, because he believes himself to be that which, in fact, he is not. Man is neither form, feeling, perception, tendency nor consciousness, but when he considers himself to be these things there arises the illusion of personality, and he becomes subject to a limitation which is productive of fear, misery and hatred. For in attaching himself to qualities he makes himself their slave, and is therefore compelled to react to their fortunes or misfortunes, while in his true state he is above and beyond them—indeed he is That which makes them possible. Why should he remain a slave?

Omai

But we are liable here to become entangled in words. Does it all come to this? We must look to the purpose of our day's activity, and that of the littlest deed, and then examine the reason for doing it, our motive for the act. Only thus shall we reach the perfect act, and 'the perfect act has no result', because there is no self left to receive it. We may understand this better when we come to the universal Law of Karma, the living and intelligent Law of Harmony which judges every action and its motive, and accords the right result. Meanwhile let us attempt to do right 'in the scorn of consequence'.

ONE FOND OFFENCE

Study this penetrating phrase of Edwin Arnold:

Enter the path. There is no grief like hate!
    No pains like passion, no deceit like sense!

Enter the path. Far hath he gone whose foot
Treads down one fond offence.

The Light of Asia

IT HAS BEEN SAID

Nothing is good which cannot be destroyed.

From the Chinese

It is not how good you are that matters, but what good are you?

Honesty is the best policy, but he who acts on that principle is not an honest man.

The difficult is that which can be done immediately, the impossible that which takes a little longer.

Nansen

STUDY PRINCIPLES

A person, on being assured that he would certainly one day enjoy an adequate competence if he closely followed the industrious habit of the thrifty bee, spent the greater part of his life in anointing his thighs with the yellow powder which he laboriously collected from the flowers of the field. Learn, therefore, that wisdom lies in an intelligent perception of great principles, and not in the slavish imitation of details.

E. Bramah

TAIL PIECE

THINGS ARE WHAT THEY ARE

There is a famous Zen story which may be applied to one's life at frequent intervals.

Two monks on the way home came to a ford, and found waiting there a pretty girl in her best clothes hesitating to get them wet in crossing. The first monk, hardly breaking step, picked her up in his arms and carried her over. She thanked him and the two men went on their way. After about two miles the second monk could contain himself no longer. 'How could you do that, taking a girl in your arms. You know the Rules . . .' and much more to this effect. Said the first monk with a smile, 'You must be tired, carrying the girl all this way. I put her down at the ford.'

R. H. Blyth comments, 'Things are beautiful but not desirable; ugly but not repulsive; false but not rejected; dirty but ourselves no cleaner'. In brief, they are what they are. The rest is our own addition. So, he might add, freedom lies in accepting our limitations.

But surely there is much more in this delightful story, quoted in every work on Zen, than these remarks of R. H. Blyth? At least four other 'morals' have been suggested. Choose your own and make use of it.

QUESTIONS

1 Can you now see that even at rest you are in action even though it be what you call non-action?

2 Have you discovered the enormous power of inaction in a crisis or wherever everyone else is in busy action and expecting you to do the same? Here is a potential dynamo, wasting none of its power and ready to apply it when called for, if at all.

3 What percentage of what you do in twenty-four hours is the product of habit, and what of this, on reflection, is of the least use to anyone at all, yourself included?

Theme 6

THE MIDDLE WAY BETWEEN
THE OPPOSITES

The middle way between extremes is an obvious ideal in every form of action. In Buddhism, however, it is far more, and even forms part of the First Sermon of the Buddha as recorded in the Pali Canon.

> Monks, these two extremes which should not be followed by one who has gone forth as a wanderer. What two?
> Devotion to the pleasures of sense, a practice unworthy, unprofitable, the way of the world; and devotion to self-mortification, which is painful, unworthy and unprofitable.
> By avoiding these two extremes the Tathagata [the Buddha] has gained knowledge of that middle Path which giveth vision, which giveth knowledge, which causeth calm, enlightenment. And what, monks, is that middle path which giveth vision . . .?

And the Buddha answered himself with an exposition of the famous Eightfold Path which leads from basic Right Views to the deepest form of inward spiritual insight.

These two extremes are but two of a thousand Pairs of Opposites between which we must learn to pick and choose our firm and careful way. The accent is on firm. We cannot avoid the existence of the Opposites, nor waver weakly back and forth between them.

DON'T WOBBLE

> If you walk, just walk. If you sit, just sit . . . but don't wobble.
> **The master Ummon**

In a world of duality, for such is all manifestation, these Pairs of Opposites dominate our every thought and act. From the metaphysics of Spirit/Matter to whether we drink coffee or tea for breakfast, we live in a tension of choice, and we must slowly come to terms with this situation, learning to use it and learn by it without attachment, and so far as possible without choice.

71

Let us look at the Opposites as a false reality to be used and then transcended. We see and feel the tension between them in every thought and action of the day. The highest, metaphysical pair may seem beyond our immediate grasp, but lower aspects of these two, reflected down through the planes of manifestation, may either be seen as complementary opposites to one of which we are more or less attached at the moment, or as irritating opposition to our ego-will coming from a source which, as an opponent party in politics or a rival religion, should surely be abolished!

Human and divine, male and female, action-reaction, these are obvious. In philosophy we read of subject-object, affirmation-negation, cause-effect; in psychology of the conscious and unconscious, introvert and extravert, the intellect and the intuition. In all religion we find *jiriki*, salvation by self-power and *tariki*, by 'other'-power, and in Buddhism in particular the complementary ideal of the Arhat and Bodhisattva, of Wisdom/Compassion, of the Self and Not-Self, so gravely misunderstood by those who claim that there is no self at all. In the rhythmic alternation of nature we have the cycle of growth and decay, of day and night, of work and rest, and everywhere the conflict between part and whole, of the individual and the State and the troublesome problem of good and evil. But the list is endless.

In respect of all these opposites we can lay down four propositions, not as dogma but as facts available to all who examine life for themselves.

First, each of a pair exists by virtue of the other, whether as complementary opposites like positive and negative, or comparative attributes such as large and small. This is a profound statement, but understanding of it tends to ease one out of the false position in which we stand.

It follows that each opposite is partial, incomplete, both being needed for the least expression of truth. Hence the acceptance by religions and philosophies of a relative and an absolute Truth, the former pertaining to the realm of intellectual digestion and 'proof', the latter remaining forever beyond consciousness which has not climbed to its own level of No-thought, No-Mind, in pure awareness. Even in the lower field of relative understanding this new view of the opposites will slay all dogmatism. How can any statement be the subject of worship or even of unchangeable conviction when the opposite claims attention as of equal right to be heard? And are not the opposites of 'right' and 'wrong' now suspect? At least they are relative to each other and much else.

Secondly, it does not need a profound sense of mysticism to see that each of the opposites *is* in a sense the other. At least we can see the two sides as closely as the two sides of a coin. And thirdly, each *needs* the other in order to be complete. This has profound importance in the field of psychology. Do we realize that we *need* the thing we hate, the aspects of the self we thrust into the unconscious as unworthy of the mask we offer to the world?

As a fourth proposition it is submitted that the tension inherent in duality, of attraction/repulsion working at full force on things, people and situations, is either accepted as the motive force of growth and development, or regarded as a source of suffering by those who cannot see it in this light. He who feels himself to be pushed about by the contending force between the opposites, and resents the pressure, will suffer by his resistance. But he who perceives and learns to use the flow of force to his own and the world's betterment, will feel no suffering thereby.

The extremes of cosmic tension are most severely felt within the mind. On the one hand, the Life-force, flowing from the Unborn through every form or thing or event, uses all alike to its own high purposes; on the other hand the ego-self, blind with the illusion of separate existence, and deaf to the voice of the Buddha-mind within, strives for self, and pitting its will against that of the universe is filled with suffering wrought of its purely personal desires.

THREE QUESTIONS

We can now ask ourselves three questions. In every case where one of the opposites is dominant in the mind, can we genuinely see and actually express the other point of view? I was deeply impressed to learn of a debating society where no main speaker was allowed to support one side of a controversial motion until he had satisfied the committee that he could sincerely though briefly speak to precisely the opposite. What fun, if this were the rule in the House of Commons: or even in the Buddhist Society! Could the exclusive Theravadin student argue, apparently sincerely, the delights of Zen? Or vice versa?

A second question: Can we be truly tolerant of the 'other', that blithering idiot who insists on going straight to hell with his dangerous and quite horrible ideas? Probably not, but I remember a definition of tolerance given by Annie Besant fifty years ago; 'an eager and a glad acceptance of the way along which our brother seeks the truth'. Yes, we must let him go the way he wills, and not insist on our admonishment. And a third question; can we choose and use the opposites yet not be bound by our choice? We choose all day but can we struggle free from our choosing? Probably not, for we are conditioned by our birth, sex, religion, education, environment, job and home. How difficult, then, to 'let the mind abide nowhere', said to be the greatest phrase from the East. We strive to walk on with a load of thought-creation on our backs, all the heavier for being unrecognized.

How shall we move between the opposites, avoiding all extremes?

AVOIDING ALL EXTREMES

For the Middle Way is no mere compromise, no choosing a little from each conflicting claim. It is the avoidance of *all* extremes, of living, feeling, thought or act. We must learn to realize that every attribute, be it old, hot, straight or wise, has an opposite, and at early stages of the Path we learn to choose the better of the two. Later we learn that the difficult choice in discovering our Dharma is not between right and wrong but between the more right and the less right in the circumstances. Truly the path of duty is 'narrow as a razor's edge'. But the problem is more subtle still, for the Middle Way is not so much between as *above* these countless Pairs of Opposites, a state of consciousness in which life is lived without personal reaction of any vehement kind, without violent likes and dislikes, or the objective labelling of things and acts and other people as good or bad. The root of illusion and hence of evil is the discriminative mind, and so long as we view all things as either this *or* that, regarding all things from a personal point of view, so long shall we view as twofold that which is only One.

Not till we drop the habit of calling all things by the name of some extreme shall we enter the Path which knows of neither. The Middle Way is trodden at a level of consciousness where every attribute is seen to be true at the moment, but not later or before, right here but not necessarily there, proper for this man but not perhaps for that. On such a plane discriminative judgement is never exercised against another's act or motive unless the circumstances call imperatively for such a judgement to be made. 'Judge not that ye be not judged'. Judge not others lest the karmic effects of your interference return unwanted to your door.

The tension of the opposites within us creates of course a host of problems, large and small.

PROBLEMS

The greatest and most important problems in life are all fundamentally insoluble. They must be so, because they express the necessary polarity inherent in every self-regulating system. They can never be solved, but only outgrown.

From Carl Jung's Commentary in *The Secret of the Golden Flower*

But Jung had much more to say on problems.

I always worked with the temperamental conviction that in the last analysis there were no insoluble problems, and I have often seen individuals who simply outgrew a problem which had destroyed others. This 'outgrowing' revealed itself to be the raising of the level of consciousness. Some higher or wider interest arose on the person's horizon, and through the widening of his view the insoluble problem lost its urgency. It was not solved logically in its own terms, but faded out in contrast to a new and stronger life-tendency. It was not repressed and made unconscious, but merely appeared in a different light, and so became different itself.

This memorable passage from Jung's Commentary on *The Secret of the Golden Flower* is a most interesting rediscovery of an ancient truth, long known in the East as 'the higher third'. As Truth makes a higher third of truth and untruth, the Good above both good and evil, and Beauty above the ugly and the beautiful, so above every of the Pairs of Opposites is, on the plane of Non-duality, in raised consciousness a vision of that which unites the two.

This widening of view is concerned with great virtues. The first is Tolerance, one of the supreme virtues of Buddhism where its universal presence is unique among the world's religions. Where else can one read of the Founder of a religion speaking as follows?

TOLERANCE

So, then, Kālāmas, as to my words to you just now: 'Be ye not misled by proficiency in the collections [of Scriptures], nor by mere logic or inference, nor after considering reasons, nor after reflection on and approval of some theory, nor because it fits becoming, nor out of respect for the recluse (who holds it). But, Kālāmas, when you know for yourselves: These things are unprofitable, these things are blameworthy, these things are censured by the intelligent; these things, when performed and undertaken, conduct to loss and sorrow—then indeed do ye reject them', such was my reason for uttering those words.

Come now, Kālāmas, be ye not . . . so misled. But if at any time ye know of yourselves: These things are profitable, they are blameless, they are praised by the intelligent; these things, when performed and undertaken, conduct to profit and happiness— then, Kālāmas, do ye, having undertaken them, abide therein.

From: *The Kālāma Sutra* of the Pali Canon

HUMOUR

There is something wrong with the man who does not laugh. And the fact that life is hard for him, at the moment or always, is no cause for perpetual solemnity. In the West we have a Christian tradition that religion is a solemn affair, and at one time it was held one should not joke on Sundays. At the other extreme, I have seldom heard such a quantity and quality of honest 'belly' laughter as when staying in a Rinzai Zen monastery in Japan.

SOLEMNITY

Woe to the philosophers who cannot laugh away their learned wrinkles. I look on Solemnity as a disease. It appears to me that Morality, Study and Gaiety are three sisters, who should never be separated.

Voltaire

It has long been said that a man who fears does not laugh, and that he who laughs at all things, himself most of all, as distinct from the silly giggle of the empty mind, is a man who is unafraid. The rabid egotist, the criminal mind who is an enemy to society, will seldom laugh, save at some other person. But true laughter is not unkind. It is an expression of heart's ease and an inner balance. Such a man meets sorrow as it comes, and all the other feeling which cause furrows on the faces of the passer-by. Let him lift in consciousness and be the less affected by all the world's affairs which are not his concern nor his to help.

THE LAUGHING WAY

A 'jest' is essentially non-relative, and its reaction is—laughter! Might we not do well, and wisely, to proclaim it as the Way—as our Way at least? Even Nietzsche, a sage in his very particular 'way', named one of his works 'The Joyful Wisdom'.

At least it can be asserted that solemnity as such is not, and never could be, any sort or kind of a 'way' out of the manifest absurdity of Relativity!

And what more potent detergent is known to us than LAUGHTER? Solemnity, surely, never rid anyone of any malady, physical or psychic: it may be ecclesiastic but quite certainly it is not spiritual. Religious, it might perhaps be, but then the word 'religion' can only mean what it says—and that is 're-binding'.

I have just pointed out that the essence of a joke is non-relative and thereby immediately indicates Absolute. If we knew that, might we not *look* instead of ceasing-to-look and so falling directly into our conditioned habit of 'seeing' something or conceiving something? Then our 'looking'—which is purely Subjective— might, indeed should, hold the necessary temporal split-second just long enough to allow what-is-looking to survive the objective 'seeing', which is conceiving and bondage.

We should then *be* the joke, and we would laugh into the Subjectivity which is what-we-ARE. Might such not be *The Laughing Way*?

Wei Wu Wei

He who laughs knows the faults of others as brother to his own. Accepting all, he radiates his inward happiness.

FAULT-FINDING

He who treads the path in earnest
Sees not the mistakes of the world;
If we find fault with others
We ourselves are also in the wrong

From *The Sutra of Hui-neng*

IT HAS BEEN SAID

Avoid extremes, but don't be extreme in your avoidance.

Progress is in a rhythmic alternation of unbalance.
(I devised this sentence on noticing a long time ago the profoundly important fact that man walks upon two legs. May I suggest that you ponder upon this profound discovery?)

A heart untouched by worldly things, a heart that is not swayed By sorrow, this is the greatest blessing.

The Sutta Nipata

THE HIGHER THIRD

Is the solution to all problems arising from tension between the Opposites to seek and climb to a Higher Third, not between them but above them? Making the apex of a triangle from which in consciousness we can look down on each of the pairs? A strange awareness follows. We speak of truth and falsehood, but there is

Truth higher than and including both; of the beautiful and the ugly, but some have seen the Beauty which encompassed both; good and evil and a Good in which they are seen as the two sides of a coin.

This Higher Third is the true Middle Way between the Opposites, for it resolves them as such. In the world we choose a hundred times a day, but now we know that we choose and that the other of the two is equally true/untrue, good/bad. In terms of metaphysics, of which the Western mind is notoriously wary, the Absolute or Buddha-mind, being the source of duality is of course above and beyond all pairs, and each of all pairs is lop-sided. This is at least an interesting thought when we next find ourselves involved in a heated argument, and defending an extreme point of view! For what applies to metaphysics, the world of cosmic principles, applies here below—and everywhere.

AS ABOVE, SO BELOW

> As is the Inner so is the Outer; as is the Great so is the Small; as it is Above so it is Below; there is but one Life and Law. Nothing is Inner, nothing is Outer; nothing is Great, nothing is Small; nothing is High, Nothing is Low, in the Divine Economy
>
> Source unknown

This Higher Third existed, then, long before the twin Opposites which it enfolds. The Two came from the One which came from the Unborn Absolute, which the Hindus so wisely call THAT. Let us then look at a specimen of this Higher Third, even as we considered 'Life is One' as an example of Thought-force, or cosmic concept, when examining Theme Two.

SAY NOT THAT BEAUTY

> Say not that beauty is an idle thing . . .
> For 'tis not so. Through dedicated days
>   And foiled adventure of deliberate nights
> We lose and find and stumble in the ways
>   That lead to the far confluence of delights.
> Not with the earthly eye and fleshly ear
>   But lifted far above mortality

We see at last the eternal hills, and hear
  The sighing of the universal sea;
And kneeling breathless in the holy place
  We see immortal Beauty face to face.

Robin Flower

Of course 'all beauty lies in the beholder's eye' that is, in the mind, as all else, but so does the beholder's reaction to what he sees. It is for him to decide his response to nakedness, in life or in art, or to the rhythm of the tom-tom. And may he not let his heart/mind be raised by what to him is great beauty, whether man-made or of Nature? Has any man become the more sense-bound by great music, great art of any kind as generally so accepted?

And does not a mind attuned to beauty begin to see in unexpected places the reflection of this seemingly divine glory? Have you ever seriously considered, for example, the unique sleek blackness of the face of a piece of coal? Or, if coal be hard to come by in these days, the many-greened elaborate convolutions of a cabbage (only a rose in form but larger and of a different colour!)? Or made a close examination, as she rests on your hand, of a blow-fly? You may laugh, but others have noticed these things. And is the soft 'susurration' of the falling tide on a shingle beach not equal in its own terms to the 'three B's' of Western music, when the mind is suitably attuned to its different wave-length?

But enough of personal opinion. Let us read what others have said before meditating on the inmost meaning of Beauty.

BEAUTY

And we walked together, I that am I and I that am not I, and the hand of Beauty lay upon the waking dawn. Before us rose the mountains, mantled with an unstained purity; beneath us at our feet, the fertile valley redolent with sleepy-headed flowers; while in the distance, in the hollow of the immemorial hills, lay the wide spaces of the sea. We paused awhile upon our way, and the world was still. Man was not, and the scene was beautiful, even as I that am I. But elsewhere, ran the current of my thought, presumptuous man has placed on Nature's handiwork the fretful finger of his immaturity, and all is harsh, imperfect, and of a most distasteful crudity, even as I that am not I. Wherefore it seems to me that this frail flower at my feet is more myself than all the cold magnificence of men. Is not the flower of the field the image of our own evolving life? See how it welcomes all that comes, or wet or fine, or cold or warm, bowing to all, resisting nothing. Yet through the changing fortunes of the day it grows unceasingly towards a swift perfection that was preordained. Yet man is surely greater than the flower. I must think upon these things.

From the meditations of Komo Ki

FELLOWSHIP WITH THE LOVELY

Then the venerable Ananda came to the Exalted One, saluted him, and sat down at one side. So seated, the venerable Ananda said:

'The half of the holy life, Lord, is the friendship with what is lovely, association with what is lovely, intimacy with what is lovely'.

'Say not so, Ananda! Say not so, Ananda! It is the whole not the half of the holy life. Of a brother so blessed with fellowship with what is lovely we may expect this, that he will develop the Ariyan Eightfold Path, that he will make much of the Ariyan Eightfold Path.'

From the Pali Canon

Yet this is still perhaps mere beauty, and the truly awakened eye must learn to see 'suddenly', with the eye of intuition, the glory of a tree, or sunset which stills mere speech, or the heart-lifting splendour which fills the soul on entering a great cathedral. I choose these examples at random from my own experience, but it must be 'seeing' in which self has vanished, in which there is no longer 'I' to see, when trivial distinctions of form and colour and comparison have died away and Beauty is nakedly revealed.

Meditate I pray you on Eva Gore-Booth's incredible couplet in her 'Reincarnation', and digest its quite enormous implications.

BECAUSE OF PRIMROSES

Because of primroses, time out of mind
The Lonely turns away from the Alone . . .

From 'Reincarnation'. Eva Gore-Booth

Study it again. For the part, the infinitely trivial part, it may be of you or me, the arrow-journey to our own divinity for a single flower's divine magnificence, and suddenly to *see* . . .

I CANNOT DIE WHILE BEAUTY CALLS

I cannot die while beauty calls.
The body fails, and in the quiet heart
Some measure lies, some sense, of duty done.
And yet, while set and girded to depart
I see, as though a light through fading walls
Of earth, these glimpses of the final sun.
I needs must live awhile, nor wonder why.
While beauty calls I cannot die.

True loveliness in every form,
To every sense and tentacle of mind
Is boldly visible, a shouting claim
Of certainty for eyes not beauty-blind.
It sings and glows and soft enfolds the warm
Entirety of all that bears a name.

Oh, glory of the earth and sky!
While so much beauty calls I cannot die.

T. C. H.

QUESTIONS

1 Have you found in yourself a sense of beauty, as a quality of life of value equal to the true or the good? If not, does its absence trouble you?

2 'Beauty dwells in the beholder's eye'. True or false?

3 Fashions in art change constantly. Are there any constants of Beauty which do not change?

4 Is there beauty of character or mind as well as of form and sound?

5 Have you ever *seen* a flower, a tree, a butterfly?

Theme 7
KARMA, THE LAW OF HARMONY

The twin doctrines of Karma and Rebirth first became known to the Western mind through the writings of H. P. Blavatsky. This great writer was trained in Tibet for many years before being sent by her Master to publish in the West an outline of the immemorial Wisdom of mankind, 'the accumulated wisdom of the ages', concerning cosmogenesis, the periodic manifestation of the Absolute, and anthropogenesis, the birth of man, his nature, evolution and glorious destiny. Having published much of this in *The Secret Doctrine* (1888), in 1889 she wrote a simpler exposition of this Theosophy, and herein makes plain the total range of the ultimate Law, in the East called Karma, the inevitable corollary of which is the doctrine of Rebirth.

Karma she describes as 'the Ultimate Law of the Universe, the source, origin and fount of all other laws which exist throughout Nature. Karma is the unerring law which adjusts effect to cause, on the physical, mental and spiritual planes of being. As no cause remains without its due effect from greatest to least, from a cosmic disturbance down to the movement of your hand, and as like produces like, Karma is that unseen and unknown law which adjusts wisely, intelligently and equitably each effect to its cause, tracing the latter back to its producer. Though itself unknowable its action is perceivable.'

Note that the law is intelligent, for this is in accord with the occult doctrine that all is alive and nothing dead, not even a law. There are living entities, call them what you will, from the highest 'gods' to the lowest crystal, and whether the form be visible to the human eye is immaterial. A living law is an exciting thought, and with deep meditation may solve much that we do not now understand of 'guardian angels', 'forces of Fate', good and bad 'luck', and much beside. But if Karma as a law be true there is no more chance or luck or coincidence to aggravate or help our lives; only a total harmony, the breaking of which is a bill which the breaker must in this life, or some other, pay.

As I wrote in my *Karma and Rebirth* (1942), 'Karma is a Law which dominates all other natural laws, from gravity to the law of averages, but it is not blind Law. It is living and intelligent as all else in the universe. "There is no such thing as either 'dead' or 'blind' matter, as there is no 'blind' or 'unconscious' Law, for the Universe is worked and guided from within outwards. As above, so it is below, as in heaven so on earth; and man, the microcosm and miniature copy of the macrocosm, is the living witness to this Universal Law, and to the mode of its action."' The quotation is from *The Secret Doctrine* by H. P. Blavatsky.

KARMA, THE LAW OF HARMONY

The key-word is indeed harmony, as may be seen from these two further quotations. As H. P. Blavatsky wrote in *The Secret Doctrine*,

> The only decree of Karma, an eternal and immutable decree, is absolute Harmony in the world of Matter as in the world of Spirit. It is not, therefore, Karma that rewards or punishes, but it is we who reward and punish ourselves, according as we work with and through Nature, abiding by the laws on which that Harmony depends, or breaking them.

THE WEB

> Constantly picture the universe as a living organism, controlling a single substance and a single soul, and note how all things react upon a single world sense, all act by a single impulse, and all co-operate towards all that comes to pass; and mark the contexture and concatenation of the web.

Marcus Aurelius

PURPOSE AND DESIGN

> The Law of Karma seems to display full purpose and design, a relation of cause/effect between all persons and indeed between all units of manifestation of the one inseverable Life-force. If this be so, the fact of unceasing changes now ratified by science should no longer be viewed as a matter for regret but as a process of perpetual, purposeful Becoming under law, which regulates the

incidence of cause/effect in a way in which we can intelligently take at least a limited part. Moreover, the law may be seen as an aspect of the Life-process itself, and as such both living and intelligent. This is a bold concept, but a grasp of it illumines the whole field of our Becoming. Karma can now be seen as the servant of what Sir Edwin Arnold called 'the power divine which moves to good; only its laws endure'. It is also the will of God, if God be viewed as Buddha-Mind, Dharma incarnate. We need no longer rail at 'change and decay in all around I see', as the hymn has it; we can accept the law of change and find it 'rightly so'. By acceptance we can understand the workings of the Law, and use it to the gain of all that lives.

Santana

RESTORING THE LEVEL

In a famous passage from his *Lectures and Biographical Sketches* (1868) Emerson wrote,

If you love and serve men, you cannot by any hiding or stratagem escape the remuneration. Secret retributions are always restoring the level, when disturbed, of the divine justice. It is impossible to tilt the beam. All the tyrants and proprietors and monopolists of the world in vain set their shoulders to heave the bar. Settles for evermore the ponderous equator to its line, and man and mote, and star and sun must range to it, or be pulverized by the recoil.

The Law is, of course, immensely complicated.

Wonderful, Lord! How deep is this causal Law, and how deep it seems. And yet do I regard it as plain to understanding.

Say not so, Ananda! Deep indeed is this causal Law. It is by not understanding, by not penetrating this doctrine that this world of men has become entangled like a ball of twine, and unable to pass beyond the Ceaseless Round (of Rebirth).

The Sutta Nipata of the Pali Canon

We know it already in the well-known phrase 'Cause and effect are equal and opposite', and we were taught it when young as the moral

85

retribution which follows evil acts. But it is not fatalism and should never be so regarded.

YE ARE NOT BOUND!

If ye lay bound upon the wheel of change,
    And no way were of breaking from the chain
The Heart of boundless being is a curse,
    The Soul of Things fell pain.
Ye are not bound! the Soul of Things is sweet,
    The Heart of Being is celestial rest;
Stronger than woe is will; that which was Good
    Doth pass to Better——Best.

The Light of Asia

For our reaction to any event or situation is, always allowing for the bondage created by our past karma, for us to decide.

TRUE

The Moving Finger writes; and, having writ
Moves on; nor all thy Piety nor Wit
    Shall lure it back to cancel half a Line
Nor all thy Tears wash out a Word of it.

Omar Khayyam

But we are still as free as we have left ourselves.

WE MAKE OUR OWN MISFORTUNES

'His son is dead.' What has happened? 'His son is dead.' Nothing more? 'Nothing'. 'His ship is lost.' What has happened? 'His ship is lost.' 'He has been haled to prison.' What has happened? 'He has been haled to prison.'

But that any of these things are misfortunes to him is an addition which everyone makes of his own.

Epictetus

THE SOURCE OF HAPPINESS

We all wish you happiness, but our wishes cannot give it. Nor can it come from outward circumstance. It can only come from yourselves, from the spirit that is within you. You cannot choose what changes and chances are to befall you in the coming years, but you can choose the spirit with which you will meet them.

The Archbishop of Canterbury to the then Duke and Duchess of Kent

FREEWILL

Man's free-will is but a bird in a cage; he can stop at the lower perch, or he can mount to a higher. Then that which is and knows will enlarge his cage, give him a higher and a higher perch, and at last break off the top of his cage, and let him out to be one with the free-will of the universe.

Tennyson

And our self-imposed limitations, added to those imposed by the laws of Nature, in a way create and announce our freedom.

FREEDOM

There is no freedom save under law, as many a country has discovered in terms of man-made law and order. It is therefore worthwhile considering the subject further. If you struggle to be free, from what, and who struggles? As a river is a river by virtue of the constriction of its banks—else it becomes a flat and useless puddle—so each aspect and creation of the one Life-force is what it is, and is useful and strong as it is, by virtue of the form enclosing.

Ananda

And it is all Right, not right but Right!

'All that happens happens right.' Watch closely, you will find it so. Not merely in the order of events but by scale of right, as though some power apportions all according to worth.

Marcus Aurelius

Epictetus, an equally famous Stoic, puts it more strongly still,

True instruction is this: to learn to wish that each thing should come to pass as it does.

Epictetus

Yet we must spend time in facing, examining and in a sense digesting

87

our old Karma before we are fully free to decide new action which will almost inevitably have new results.

ACTION HAS RESULT

Brethren, of deeds done and accumulated with deliberate intent I declare there is no wiping out. That wiping out has to come to pass either in this very life or in some other life at its proper occasion. Without recognition of deeds so done, brethren, I declare there is no making an end of suffering.

The Pali Canon

REDUCE OLD KARMA

According harmoniously with the conditions of your present lives, you should go on, as opportunities arise, reducing the store of the old Karma laid up in previous lives; and above all, you must avoid building up a fresh store of retribution for yourselves.

From The Zen Teaching of Huang Po

Meanwhile we must learn to control our reaction to current events, lest we create new 'unskilful' karma as the cause of suffering to come.

Let every man prove his own work, and then shall he have rejoicing in himself alone, and not in another. For every man shall bear his own burden. Be not deceived; God is not mocked, for whatsoever a man soweth that shall he also reap. For he that soweth to his flesh shall of the flesh reap corruption; but he that soweth to the Spirit shall reap life everlasting . . .

From the Letters of St Paul

He that planteth and he that watereth are one; and every man shall receive his own reward according to his own labour.

St Paul

Karma is the adjustment of effects flowing from causes, during which the being from whom and through whom that adjustment is effected experiences pleasure or pain.

W. Q. Judge

The Law is cosmic, and has been called the ultimate Law of the universe. It follows that all causes created by all men on any plane affect all other men. This is a staggering thought but nevertheless we can only fully control our own.

> Thou canst create this 'day' thy chances for thy 'morrow'. In the 'Great Journey' causes sown each hour bear each its harvest of effects, for rigid Justice rules the world. With mighty sweep of never-erring action it brings to mortal lives of weal or woe, the karmic progeny of all our former thoughts and deeds.
>
> *The Voice of the Silence*

Thus, although it is a cosmic Law, Karma as the living, intelligent, all-pervading Law of Harmony, can be intensely personal.

> 'Destiny, scowling-black, on her dark throne,
> Tangles my feet', he mourned, 'and bids me fail.'
> Then, with sad eyes, he peeped behind the veil;
> Stared at the face of fate—and saw his own.
>
> Stanton Cobling

Before attempting to understand something of what the Law implies look again at these immortal lines from Tennyson's 'Oenone'.

FROM 'OENONE'

> Self-reverence, self-knowledge, self-control.
> These three alone lead life to sovereign power.
> Yet not for power (power of herself
> Would come uncalled for), but to live by law,
> Acting the law we live by without fear.
> And, because right is right, to follow right
> Were wisdom in the scorn of consequence.
>
> Tennyson

KARMA APPLIED DESTROYS:

1 Any need for the concept of a Personal yet Almighty God.

2 The search for authority of any kind, least of all that of a Saviour who is in all things the supreme and unquestionable Authority.

3 The habit of blaming someone or something for all that comes to us as the result of our own causing.

4 Belief in luck, good or bad, chance, or coincidence. Disbelief is itself a frightening exercise, but can such things be in a universe ruled by, because it totally is, pure Harmony?

5 A sense of finality in death, of anything or anyone. For this examine Theme 8.

KARMA APPLIED CREATES:

1 The complete acceptance of all conditions and events. 'It's ALL RIGHT.'

2 The ability to stand on our own feet at all times.

3 Unlimited strength of purpose and hence the power to achieve in time awareness of Enlightenment.

IT HAS BEEN SAID

Philosophy is the only true perception and understanding of cause and effect.

Paracelsus

Every one of our physical or mental movements is the fruit of causes deriving from the whole universe, and has repercussions in the whole universe.

Alexandra David-Neel

Universal Harmony tends ever to resume its original position like a bough which, bent down too forcibly, rebounds with corresponding vigour.

H. P. Blavatsky

The cause never knows the effect; it becomes it. The effect never knows its cause; it is it.

Christmas Humphreys

It is written: 'Teach to eschew all causes; the ripple of effect, as the great tidal wave, thou shalt let run its course'.

The Voice of the Silence

In the case of human incarnations the law of Karma, racial or individual, overrides the subordinate tendencies of Heredity, its servant.

If any man be unhappy, let him know that it is by reason of himself alone.

Epictetus

The snow falls, each flake in its appropriate place.

A Zen master

QUESTIONS

1 Can you conceive the universe as a vast and total harmony maintained by a Law which manifests as interrelated cause/effect of frightening complexity?

2 Can you conceive this Law as living and intelligent, a universal force which holds the cosmic harmony entire?

3 Can you begin to live in some awareness that all you do and feel and think is a creative cause producing a like effect which ripples out—why not?—to the margin of the universe?

4 Can you accept the Buddhist truth that we are today the net result of all we have thought and felt and done in this life and in lives gone by? And that our future, in this life and in lives to come will be as we are making it now?

Theme 8
DEATH AND REBIRTH

I DEATH

To the Buddhist the death of the physical body, with its inner 'sheaths' which die with it, is merely the process opposite to birth. In brief, 'the cause of death is birth'. That which is born, whether a man or mouse, a mountain range or a concept of Government, being born, will sometime die. There are only two unknown factors in the equation, the method and the date.

Note that it is birth which is the opposite to death, not life, which has no 'opposite', and throughout the inconceivably vast period referred to in the Pali Canon as 'the unrolling and rolling-up of the worlds', is immortal. Only its infinitely varied forms, in cycles minute and vast, are born, grow, decay and die. Such is the cycle on the Buddhist Wheel of Life—and death.

These being the physical facts, what matters is the mind's attitude towards them. Is it with fear, as with those still bound in the coils of illusion? With hope, as with those long aching with incurable disease? Or with equanimity, as one who studies the laws of life and awaits, with clear objective vision, an interesting and periodic event?

It is possible 'to die before death' and thus be rid of all emotion. Such was the deliberate practice of the Japanese samurai, who trained themselves to face and conquer death before going into battle. This is what the Zen master Hakuin is referring to in his famous Song.

FROM A SONG OF MEDITATION
OF THE ZEN MASTER, HAKUIN

O young people! If death is hateful die now.
    Dying this once you will never die again.
The sorrow and bitterness of this world will become happiness.
    You are called samurai. Should you not be ready to die?
Despite brave words the samurai who has not died this once

When the crisis comes will hide or flee away . . .
He who has once died in the depths of the navel
    The spear of the master cannot touch him.
He who dying while yet alive carries out his duties—
    The arrow of the master archer is nothing to him . . .
Throw away all and die and see—
    The god of death and his demons stand bewildered.

And then the great master goes on to speak of meditation as 'the inmost secret of the knightly way'. Here is the death of self and with it the fear of death, and he who fears not death will 'die' no more.

This is not impossible to achieve for Western Buddhists who meditate upon the inevitability of death and its periodic occurrence within the 'pairs of opposites' which the awakening Self will some day rise above. As to what lies beyond, between recurrent lives, this, though amply described in the esoteric teachings of the East, is not a profitable subject for our meditation. True character is not advanced hereby, only a curiosity unanswerable with such knowledge as is at present capable of proof.

Let us see what others have said about death which may be helpful in our own meditation.

REFLECTIONS UPON DEATH

It is a widely spread belief among all the Hindus that a person's future prenatal state and birth are moulded by the last desire he may have at the time of death. But this last desire, they say, necessarily hinges on to the shape which the person may have given to his desires, passions, etc., during his past life. It is for this very reason, viz.—that our last desire may not be unfavourable to our future progress—that we have to watch our actions and control our passions and desires throughout our whole earthly career. . . .

No man dies insane or unconscious—as some physiologists assert. Even a *madman*, or one in a fit of *delirium tremens* will have his instant of perfect lucidity at the moment of death, though unable to say so to those present.

The man may often appear dead. Yet from the last pulsation,

from and between the last throbbing of his heart and the moment when the last spark of animal heat leaves the body—the *brain thinks* and the *Ego* lives in those few brief seconds his whole life over again. Speak in whispers, ye, who assist at a death-bed and find yourselves in the solemn presence of Death. Especially have you to keep quiet just after Death has laid her clammy hand upon the body. Speak in whispers, I say, lest you disturb the quiet ripple of thought, and hinder the busy work of the Past casting its reflection upon the Veil of the Future. . . .

The good and pure sleep a quiet blissful sleep, full of happy visions of earth-life, and have no consciousness of being already for ever beyond that life. Those who were neither good nor bad, will sleep a dreamless, still and quiet sleep; while the wicked will in proportion to their grossness suffer the pangs of a nightmare lasting years; their thoughts become living things, their wicked passions—real substance, and they receive back on their heads all the misery they have heaped upon others. Reality and *fact* if described would yield a far more terrible *Inferno* than even Dante had imagined!

The Mahatma Letters to A. P. Sinnett

BIRTH-AND-DEATH

This question of birth-and-death is indeed a momentous one.

Hui-neng

This birth-and-death within the ambit life
Is utterly momentous. Form is born
And with it separation, tension, strife,
The vast illusion of division torn
From Non-duality. Yet One is two;
All form is also void. And Two is one;
No opposite but needfully must woo
Its other, though of other there is none.

We live in forms which life wills to destroy,
Their cycle ended, drawing back their breath.
And thus released we once again enjoy
The deep and thoughtful quietude of death.

T. C. H.

There came to me one who said, I fear to die. And I said, who dies? And he was silent and I said: Fear itself must die for him who understands.

Who dies, he asked me, if not I?

The body dies, I answered, but in the next life he who wears it now will wear another. The mind part perishable, part infinite, lives on. As the shrine of hatred, lust and illusion it is doomed to die, though slowly, in the lives to come. But love and truth and beauty will not die, and where the mind has neither shrine nor welcome for them, who would strive to live?

But I am I, he said, whatever the form and substance of the I, and I am fearful.

The I that is truly I is deathless, I replied. Only the I that is not I will perish and be seen no more.

Your words have the seeming of truth, he said, and may be true. Yet how shall I know that they are true, I that fear to die? The lamp knows the light, I answered, though the mirror knows it only by its power to receive. Let the light shine.

And he looked at me, and after a while I saw the dawn-light in his eyes. His words were slow, but heavy with a new born understanding. I am, he said, and am not. So, I answered him. Therefore at death you live and die.

And fear dwells in the perishable I, he mused aloud. And doubt, I said, and anger born of fear, and low desire for the I that is not I, and all illusion. So, he said, and he smiled as the sun at morning. I fear and yet I do not fear to die.

From the meditations of Komo Ki

FEAR AND DEATH

I think it strange that Death should find
So large an altar in the human mind.
Are those who die, when Birth again draws near
Filled with the same intolerable fear?
We know but Life; there's nothing dies;
Life and a walking on with opening eyes.

The body as a tree must rise and fall;
It falls and rises; should we fear at all?
T. C. H.

What, then, of the doctrine of Rebirth and, if true what is it that is again and again reborn? Let us first consider some further views on death.

IT HAS BEEN SAID

The basic cure of all life's ills is to be found in right relationship with death.

Graham Howe

Death is psychologically just as important as birth and, like this, is an integral part of life.

Carl Jung in *The Secret of the Golden Flower*

Not death is to be feared but fear of death.

Epictetus

Death is certain to all things which are born, and rebirth to all mortals, wherefore it does not behove thee to grieve about the inevitable.

The Bhagavad Gita

When death comes there is nothing more that you can do.
You fold your hands and go where you have always been.

Sokei-an Sasaki

This is profound for you should never forget where you have always been.

It is well to remember that all that bears our name is in a state of constant dissolution, and on its death will be by all but a few in a matter of months forgotten.

'BE ABSOLUTE FOR DEATH'

In Shakespeare's *Measure for Measure*, Claudio says:

The miserable have no other medicine
But only hope.
I have hope to live, and am prepared to die!

But the Duke, rejecting this relativity, answers:

Be absolute for death: either death or life
Shall thereby be the sweeter.

From *Zen in English Literature*. R. H. Blyth

QUESTIONS

1 Are you afraid of death, and if so have you noted down the reasons for your fear?

2 When you speak of death, what are you talking about, the death of what?

3 If all that dies is a form or forms—which must die sometime—does death now trouble you as it did, in your dear friend's death or the prospect of your own?

4 How do your ideas of death work in with your acceptance of rebirth?

II   REBIRTH

So much for death of the body and, according to the ancient Wisdom, several more of the finer sheaths of the complex Self. What is reborn, if anything? This Course avoids debatable doctrine as far as possible but let us assume, as a reasonable hypothesis, that the mass of causes in the mind at death which have not yet reached their effect do not dissolve, nor, as some have suggested, flow back into the vast reservoir of the manifest Cosmos. They reappear, reborn at some time and place, in a new set of vehicles or clothing to resume the long pilgrimage to Enlightenment. At least this proposition makes sense, is utterly just and is merely following at a higher level the 'round of rebirth' observable in nature.

What, then, is reborn? The Christians call it soul. So be it, but it is certainly not immortal. On the contrary, it seems like every other single 'thing' in existence, to be changing rapidly every second of time. When I read, in 1918, Ananda Coomaraswamy's *Buddha and the Gospel of Buddhism* I noted that he called it character, and this seems an admirable term for it. Look again at Theme 2 and study the make-up of the complex Self. We can ignore the body and its psychic counterpart, alike dissolved at death, and we can equally ignore the Atman, the flame of the Light of pure Spirit which is not yours or mine but is inherent in every form. The same applies to its vehicle in the individual, Buddhi as called in the East, the intuition. This leaves the mind, higher and lower as we have called it, and *kama*, the level or wave-length or vehicle of desire, itself complex, for it is at once the seat of our animal passion and self-ish desires and yet the valve, as I like to term it, for the intake of cosmic energy, including that curious form of energy we call emotion.

As Lao-Tzu, the Founder of Taoism, truly said, great characters are never built in a few years, yet the character is the man, as Dr Suzuki more than once made clear. It has been called 'a recognition of values and the power to act in accordance with one's choice'. Its constituents themselves produce a highly complex aggregate of changing factors, together the end-product of lives of Karma, the effects of causes, all constantly affected by new experience, reaction to it and self-training. All are suffused with emotion/desire, high and low in tension between the Opposites, and the whole bundle is confronted at all times with situations, major and minor, and with other 'characters'. It is essentially dual, with, as it were, a valve in the middle through which mind is rising to Mind, producing what we may accept as a God-animal. But man is equally torn between self and the other forms of Self about him or laterally, and the double tension places him firmly on—a Cross.

With the details of the reborn temporary 'entity' we are not, it must be repeated, here concerned, but it is a mighty conglomeration of powers and faculties, covering in a sense the whole man from Spirit to matter, and the paradox must now be faced that it is at once entirely separate, a being or thing of its own somewhere on the path to the mountain top, and yet inseverably, utterly one with all other Selves or characters or reincarnating 'entities'.

When this is digested it will be seen that an understanding of Rebirth, at least as a process however it works in detail, profoundly affects our attitude to life here and now, and our plans for the future.

Rebirth is an immensely old and wide belief, and is surely the inevitable corollary of Karma, for if it is *not* true the universe, which seems such an intricate conjunction of infinitely woven cycles, is sheer chaos. With its twin doctrine of Karma, Rebirth proved immediately attractive to the Western mind, whether presented in its Theosophical, Hindu or Buddhist guise. It was certainly accepted as basic Buddhism. Thus in the Pali Canon,

THE BUDDHA'S MEMORY OF PAST LIVES

I, brethren, when I so desire it, can call to mind my various states of birth, for instance one birth, two births . . a hundred thousand births; the various destructions of aeons, the various renewal of aeons, thus: I lived there, was named thus, was of such a clan, of such a caste, was thus supported, had such and such pleasant and painful experiences, had such a length of days, disappeared thence and arose elsewhere. There, too, I lived, was named thus, was of such a clan . . . (as before); thus can I call to mind in all their details, in all their characteristics in many various ways, my previous states of existence.

From the Pali Canon

Man, at birth, is the resultant of past causes of his own creation, the outcome of his actions, which are in turn the outcome of his thought, for man is the product of his thought, as is set out in the first verse of the *Dhammapada*. But subject to the limitations imposed upon his actions by the previous exercise of his will, his will is still free to create fresh causes, and thereby to modify the total effect. Thus from the moment of birth we begin to modify our circumstances, and according to our strength of will, to modify and remould our surroundings 'nearer to the heart's desire'. If we complain that circumstances are too strong for us we admit two things, first that we have so exercised our will in lives gone by that we are now entangled in a mesh of our own weaving, and secondly that we have never developed the will to the point where, to a large extent, it can rise superior to circumstance and create environment, where the weaker man is still its slave. In brief, our circumstances form the field of operations for our life's work, being collectively our Karma incarnate, but the wise man who is a strong man changes his field at will. But circumstances are not all material, and if we complain that we have no opportunity for improvement, rise my brothers! I say, and create them at your will, remembering that a neglected opportunity causes a dangerous delay.

As we study the Karmic Law we learn to control it, and by its control and exercise we create our destiny and that of all mankind. From this Right Action comes Right Inaction, the power to perform that duty which is one's Karma of the moment in the only manner which bears no Karmic progeny—impersonally. If there is that which must be done, do it with all thy might, because it must be done, indifferent to reward or punishment, remembering that the goal of all personal effort is towards the impersonal, until, with all desire purified and the fetters of self set free, one reaches the goal of all endeavour, a perfect union with all Life in full self-consciousness, and becomes, for such is the awful and yet tremendous end, 'a mere beneficent force in nature', when 'the dewdrop slips into the Shining Sea'.

THE NEW BEING

If you ask a learned Buddhist priest, what is Karma?—he will tell you that it is that cardinal tenet which teaches that as soon as any conscious or sentient being dies, a new being is produced, and he or it reappears in another birth under conditions of its own or its own antecedent making. Or, in other words that Karma is the guiding power, and Trishna (in Pali Tanha) the thirst or desire to sentiently live—the proximate force or energy, the resultant of human or animal action which, out of the old *skandhas* produce the new group that form the new being and control the nature of the birth itself. Or, to make it still clearer, the new being is rewarded and punished for the meritorious acts and misdeeds of the old one . . .

The Master K.H. in *The Mahatma Letters to A. P. Sinnett*. Letter XVI

101

Or, in a well-known verse paraphrase of the Bhagavad Gita,

REBIRTH

Nay, but as when one layeth
    His worn-out robes away,
And, taking new ones, sayeth,
    'These will I wear today',
So putteth by the spirit
    Lightly its garb of flesh
And passeth to inherit
    A residence afresh.

> From *The Song Celestial*
> of Sir Edwin Arnold

A CREED

I hold that when a person dies
    His soul returns again to earth;
Arrayed in some new flesh-disguise
    Another mother gives him birth.
With sturdier limbs and brighter brain
    The old soul takes the roads again . . .

> John Masefield

SLAVE OR PRINCE

Who toiled a slave may come anew a Prince
For gentle worthiness and merit won;
Who ruled a king may wander earth in rags
For things done and undone.

> *The Light of Asia*

The man whose devotion has been broken off by death goeth to the regions of the righteous where he dwells for an immensity of years, and is then born again on earth in a pure and fortunate family, or even in a family of those who are spiritually illumined. But such a rebirth as this last is more difficult to obtain. Being thus born again he comes in contact with the knowledge which belonged to him in his former body, and from that time he struggles for perfection more diligently. For even unwittingly, by reason of that past practice he is led and works on.

The Bhagavad Gita

THE LINK WITH KARMA

The link with Karma is of course strong. We are perpetually reborn until past causes are fully accepted and digested, and if we wish to avoid what for most is inevitable rebirth, we must work out all past causes and then learn to act impersonally, motiveless, with no self-motive now involved. There will then be nothing still bound upon the Wheel of Rebirth, not even self to be merged in Self and then SELF, for self will be ideally merged once more, and consciously with Buddha-Mind.

These are high matters, but exciting in the meditation hour. Even though as a doctrine it cannot be scientifically 'proved' it has great value in our Course. Why?

1 It opens doors to the future. We now have all the 'time' needed for the process of Enlightenment. Death is not the end; only a change of vehicle for the driver in need of a new car! It therefore kills our fear, if we have any left, of the death of the body.

2 It explains, as nothing else, the inequalities and gross injustice of our birth, the cripple, the genius, the infant prodigy. Why? Heredity alone fails utterly to give satisfaction to the mind. Why are we each so different unless we made ourselves so with our own past actions and, above all, with lives of 'thoughtless thinking'?

WATCH THOUGHTS AGAIN

Each thought is of definite length. It does not last for over what we may call an instant, but the time of its duration is in fact much shorter. It springs into life and then it dies: but it is at once reborn in the form of another thought. And thus the process goes on from moment to moment, from hour to hour, from day to day. And each one of these reincarnated thoughts lives its life, some good, some bad, some so terrible in their nature that if we could see them we would shrink back in affright. Further than that, a number of these thoughts form themselves into a certain idea, and it dies to be reincarnated in its time. Thus rolls on this vast flood. Will it overwhelm us? It may; it often does. Let us then make our thoughts pure. Our thoughts are the matrix, the mine, the fountain, the source of all that we are and of all that we may be.

W. Q. Judge

3 It strengthens the sense of Purpose for the whole incarnation, for even as we thought-created our present life so we plan the next. If it is true that between lives we digest in the heaven world of *devachan* the lessons of the life gone by, we shall exhibit the result when next reborn, in one sex and place and condition or another.

4 Whether we enter the next life 'trailing clouds of glory' as Wordsworth suggests, or not, we shall be entirely what we have made ourselves, so why not begin choosing, and creating, now?

WHEN I AM DEAD

When I am dead, who dies, who dies,
And where am I?
A dewdrop in a shining sea,
    An inmate of the sky?
Or do I rest awhile and thence
Return for new experience?

There's nothing changeless, heaven or hell
    Nor life's oblivion;
Only a heart at rest and then
    A further walking on.
We live and as we live we learn;
We die, and then again return.

Yet who returns, what comes again
    To fretful earth?
I know not. Only this I know:
There is a road that comes to birth
In every man, and at the end
Shall brother know all life as friend.

From *Exploring Buddhism.* Christmas Humphreys

QUESTIONS

1 Do you clearly accept the process of rebirth, of *some* parts of our present self or Self as a necessary corollary of the doctrine of Karma? If not, how else do you conceive the universe?

2 If you do accept rebirth, have you plans for your next life at least as clear as your personality's 'retirement'.

3 Do you see that these questions are not to test your views on doctrine, but the adoption of ideas which, as living forces in the mind, will profoundly affect your life?

Theme 9

DHARMA, THE LAW OF SERVICE

DHARMA AND KARMA

The word Dharma (*Pali*, Dhamma) has many meanings, one being commensurate with the modern term Buddhism, meaning the teaching of the Buddha. From another point of view the word means Duty, in the sense of the field of work appropriate to an individual. Such a field of duty, however, is not God-given, nor attached to the individual by any outside power. It is self-assumed, because self-created. This aspect of Dharma therefore equates with one conception of Karma, using this latter term to cover all cause-effect on every plane as affecting the individual. Such Karma must be considered subjectively and objectively, for our moods and our motorcars, our intelligence and our relatives, our trend of desire and our opportunities for its fulfilment are alike our Karma, self-induced, self-suffered or enjoyed. And, be it noted, the very fact that we 'suffer' or 'enjoy' what we are or what happens to us is an effect of our subjective Karma, that is, the quality and tendencies of our mind.

When considering Dharma in its personal application, the whole field of Karma, already examined in Theme Seven, must therefore be reviewed. One's personal Dharma includes one's choice of livelihood (however little it seems that we had the power to choose), the place and mode of our lives, and our predominant interests, and all this has been created by the self of other lives and laid before the self of this. In other words, it was chosen according to our subjective Karma to be worked out according to our objective Karma. True, the choice is within rigid limits, but these very limitations are self-induced, and for the future are being tightened or released according as our minds are expanding or contracting by their use today. The chooser of our life's Karma is the 'Self' which moves from life to life and incarnates according to the cycle of its own necessity. Wise is the man whose brain is able to discover and fulfil this destiny. As is said in *The Voice of the Silence*, 'The selfish devotee lives to no purpose. The man who does not go through his appointed work in life has lived in vain'. Yet Karma is not fatalistic. The wise man uses the path of his personal duty to expand its scope. His sole desire is to pay off every debt to life, and thereby to restore the balance he has disturbed.

If these few principles be true, it follows that one's Dharma, or field of duty in one life, is the portion of one's total Karma chosen to be then worked out. He who shirks his duty, therefore, is but putting off the day when it must be fulfilled. And this duty may be in high places or be hidden from the eyes of men; it may be hard or easy, great or small. Yet if it be one's duty it is enough that it is fulfilled. As the Japanese say:

> The pine-tree lives for a thousand years,
> The morning glory but for a single day;
> Yet both have fulfilled their destiny.

This Duty involves two principles, the payment of all debts *due*, what we *owe*, and the pursuit of that tiny part of the Plan referred to in Theme 1 which seems to us to be our Karma for this life.

Yet the path of duty, though it may as the poet has it, be the way of glory, is a hard life, with self as its constant and unremitting foe. For once it is deeply realized that Life is One, the path of duty becomes one of unceasing service, to one's fellow men, to all other forms of the same Life and, if we can rise so high in thought, to the Ultimate from which Life came.

THE CHOICE

And there came to me a young man filled with a great ideal, the service of his fellow-men, yet not unknown to bitterness. 'Long have I toiled,' he said, 'yet nothing done. For seven years I have but sought the needs of others, never of my own, and now, where is the outcome of my efforts, where the guerdon of these years of toil? Or is it foolishness to dedicate oneself to those who care not for the sacrifice?'

'My son,' I made reply, 'so that the service be pure-hearted, look not for reward. He is indeed a fool who in the service of his brothers thinks to reap their gratitude. It is enough that in the long hereafter there will come to him upon the stream of time the perfect recompense. Wise is he who is content to live by the Unserving Law, for in its arms the Yin and Yang are unified, the need of doing and the deed.

'For some there are who live by such a Law, whose lives are dedicated to its service as are those who serve a Master whom they love, as those who serve the whole of which they are a part. These have no other duties, rights or interests than helping all, according to their needs, towards Enlightenment. From deep compassion for the woes of men these fearless few have laid upon the altar of humanity all comfort, wealth, and luxury and, resolute of heart, go forth as pioneers to face the consequences of their sacrifice. Misunderstanding, persecution, utter loneliness, self-seeking, treachery, despair, all these, my son, will lie about your path, and be your sole reward. If other recompense be sought for, you will seek in vain. If it be asked of what avail this sacrifice, so alien to reason and the mind's imaginings, know that compassion comes not from the head but from the inmost chamber of the heart, which is the heart of all humanity.

'Choose, then, my son, for it is a choice which must be made. Work wisely for the welfare of men's bodies and you will reap their gratitude. Work for the mind's enlightenment and you will seek their gratitude in vain. Yet one day all will reach Enlightenment, and blessed are the few who strive to lead men to that end. Yet hearken, for the words I speak are true, such leadership is only purchased at the price of self. Choose, then, and be thoughtful in your choice, for in the realm of Law there is no compromise.'

From the meditations of Komo Ki

Some think of duty as cold and heartless, as a rather unpleasant term. It becomes when fully understood the very opposite. Service can be a total philosophy of work, which uses all day the hands of love. True, one must accept the identity of duty and service, and all that follows is based on that assumption.

SERVICE, THE PHILOSOPHY OF WORK

The world today is in a stage wherein most of us think only of ourselves.

But the Law remains, and 'Love is the fulfilling of the Law'. Man may be blind for a while, but love has never lacked a silent following to do her bidding in the world of men. But they are few, so few that each must work as never man has worked before. We do not always know to what end we work, nor why; only we know that there is work to do. Hence the futility of working for reward. Says the Bhagavad Gita: 'Thy business is with the action only, never with its fruits, so let not the fruit of action be thy motive . . . Without attachment constantly perform action which is duty, for by performing action without attachment, man verily reacheth the Supreme.' And again, in the words of a Western poet:

The game is more than the player of the game
And the ship is more than the crew.

He who would serve his fellow men must work for the sake of the work, indifferent to claims of self, of recognition or reward. He must work because the work is at hand to do, caring nought for 'merit' or the acquisition of 'good Karma,' but only that he may be a voluntary co-worker with the Universal Law.

DIGNITY

There is dignity in selfless toil, indifferent to recognition or reward. It breeds a spiritual independence, an inner poise, as different from the pandering to popular applause that marks the average man as is the night from day. The perfect server is a person motivated from within. He leads a life whose every thought and act is dedicated to a high ideal, regardless of the praise or disapproval of his fellow men.

Service is no dream. Its basis lies in appreciation of the fact that every unit of life is but an aspect of the same whole, the Oneness that men call, Reality, God, the Tao, the Absolute, Parabrahm, and a thousand other labels for the self-same concept. Hence the brotherhood of all that lives is a fact to be recognized rather than an ideal to be dragged from the realms of fancy to the life of every day.

ROMANCE

There is romance in service. Think of a handful of workers scattered throughout the countries of the world, patiently sowing the seed of centuries unborn, their every thought and word and deed to the self-same purpose dedicate, the reaping of a harvest they will never see. They reap today what unknown hands have sown, and sow in turn what other hands will reap. So that the work goes forward it matters not by whom. Our task is simple and enough for any man, to keep alight the flame of Truth, man's immemorial heritage, throughout the darkness of Kali Yuga, that when the night is past the light may be found undimmed and ready to blaze into the light of day. The spiritual forces of the world are sleeping at the present time, yet Truth will never die while there is one faithful servant left to tend its flame.

WHAT SERVICE?

What, then, is the practical philosophy of service? The task must be of our own choosing, for none can give us work to do. We must search the heart with fearless candour for the motive which controls the act, and see that it is pure. Then we must work, tirelessly, ceaselessly, that the work may be done, knowing that the more we do the less there remains for someone else to do. No server should refuse responsibility, nor leave a task undone for fear of what it will involve. If it is given us to do we must do it, immediately, and well; the strength and wisdom and material means will appear when the hour is ripe. Meanwhile look up. Laugh and be happy; for he works best who works with a cheerful heart.

Truly we live by law and are the children of our past. We are here but a short while, yet hour by hour we are moulding the lives to come. Then let us see that every act is a cause whose effect we shall welcome in a day as yet unborn, for every act that helps a brother is a fetter broken from the bonds of self. One day we shall meet Truth face to face; until then we can but tread the Path that leads to her feet, the Middle Way, whose every step is altruistic endeavour. By all means discuss, philosophize upon the Way, that the light of Truth may increasingly illumine the pitfalls at our feet, but only as they talk who tramp the self-same road together.

With hearts at peace they follow in the footsteps of the All-Compassionate One, content to sacrifice not only all they have, but even the very liberation that they hoped to gain, if only that they may more swiftly lead their brothers to the Goal which in their blindness of desire they had not seen.

Yet in the knowledge that all life is one this sacrifice becomes itself a thing of joy, for truly, as the Lama says in Talbot Mundy's *Om*, 'There is no such thing as sacrifice, there is only opportunity to serve'.

The desire to serve begins as general friendliness, and broadens into a desire and willingness to help wherever needed. This becomes in time a dedication of all available energy to a Purpose, dimly seen, beyond and above one's self, coeval with a growing awareness of Self.

This awareness in time can become one's sole and sufficient religion. It has no God and needs none. As Sir Edwin Arnold wrote,

Pray not. 'The Darkness will not brighten'. Ask
  Nought from the Silence for it cannot speak!
Vex not your mournful minds with pious pains!
  Ah! Brothers, Sisters! seek
Nought from the helpless gods by gift and hymn,
  Nor bribe with blood, nor feed with fruit and cakes;
Within yourselves deliverance must be sought;
  Each man his prison makes.

The Light of Asia

A WHOLE-TIME RELIGION

We are in action all the time, whether as planned action, reaction, non-action or at rest. Why, then, divide the day into three; work, play and religion? Why not make our action, all of it, each moment of it, our religion, using that term in the sense of a 'binding back' of the part to the Whole? This can become the 'religion of works', as it is called in the Bhagavad Gita, or total Right Action in terms of the Eightfold Path, consciously playing one's part in what seems to be the cosmic purpose, the Plan evolved by 'the Unborn' when born into the field of relativity.

Here is purpose in life, and the right motive for carrying it out, using the means convenient to the moment as a craftsman uses his tools. Every single thing we do becomes important, whether it be 'good' or comparatively 'bad'. And no effort towards right action is ever wasted, for it helped the mind to grow even if it failed. This religion is not new. For those who agree that great poetry is wisdom enshrined in the music of words, listen again to this passage from Tennyson's 'Oenone':

> Self-reverence, self knowledge, self-control,
> These three alone lead life to sovereign power.
> Yet not for power (power of herself
> Would come uncalled for), but to live by law,
> Acting the law we live by without fear.
> And, because right is right, to follow right
> Were wisdom in the scorn of consequence.

Here is new meaning in the Zen Master's answer to the pupil who asked him, 'What is Tao?' (or Reality, or Buddha-Mind). The Master replied, 'Walk on!'. Alternatively, as I described it in an article in *The Middle Way* on 'the Moving Belt of Now', we can stand and wait, relaxed yet concentrated, and watch events and situations flow towards us like moving hurdles. At the right moment, and not before, we jump them, and wait for the next!

Let us analyse an act. A deliberate, conscious act is strangely enough comparatively rare. Most of our action is reaction to outside stimulus according to habit and type of mind. If we act deliberately, to do what? With what purpose? And why do we act? If purpose is what we are trying to do, motive is why we try to do it. Right motive, as we have seen, is enormously important. In the words of the Bhagavad Gita, surely the world's finest manual of right action, 'Let the motive for action be in the action itself and not in the event'. And, again, 'he is to be esteemed who, having subdued his passions, performs with his active faculties all the duties of life unconcerned as to their result'. *Right* action is ultimately the product of indifference to self, even in well-being. There is a lovely saying, 'Make the heart empty before doing good'. Timing is the final factor. As the Arabs say, 'You cannot mount the camel that has not yet come nor the camel that has gone'. But generally speaking is there any better time for doing anything than now?

Does this sound dreary and dull? Then you are doing it wrongly.

WORK

There is no point in work
unless it absorbs you
like an absorbing game.

If it doesn't absorb you
If it's never any fun, don't do it.

D. H. Lawrence

If life for you is really going round and round on a senseless tread-mill of pleasure/pain, have another look at the Plan described in Theme 1. This, as distinct from the 'rat-race' of Western life, is serene and joyous, infinitely complex but absolutely Right, not right but RIGHT!

Learn to experience the joy of this awareness, the sense of security and certainty in all the happenings of earth and heaven. They are Law in action. They are Right. As Thoreau, the American poet, wrote, 'I know that the enterprise is worthy. I know that things work well. I have heard no bad news'.

Feel for the 'power divine' which Edwin Arnold describes; obey Polonius in his advice in *Hamlet* to Laertes,

This above all: to thine own self be true,
And it must follow as the night the day,
Thou canst not then be false to any man.

And learn obedience. To whom, to what? To the Voice of the Silence which, without the aid of words, speaks ever from within.

There is a growing awareness now of Prajna/Karuna, Wisdom/Compassion, and the oneness of the two. This is love consumed in action, so let us look again at 'the religion of works'.

There is now no more of work or play or religion as compartments of the day. We are moving now on a Way which is the perceived right purpose of the daily round. For this we need no outside Authority, however formed by the mind and however named. My own God, I like to say, is a list of the 'N.T.B.D.'—the Next Thing to be done. This is my Dharma or duty presented by my Karma of the past. This I obey, being careful that it is my duty, and not merely my selfish pleasure disguised, or interference with others' affairs in maybe the genuine belief that I know what is best for them. There is, as the Gita says, 'danger in another's duty', but *The Voice of the Silence* is equally right: 'Inaction in a deed of mercy is an action in a deadly sin'. Once more the right way is the Middle Way. All we can ask in our application of compassion is opportunity, and opportunities, as an early teacher told me, are washed up daily on your doorstep. Watch for them!

Is all this exhausting? Yes, but the next thing to be done and rightly done may be to rest. There is an alternating current of work-rest, a going out and a coming home, on cycles large and small, the largest we know being life-death and life again. Does your concept of religion need some element of asceticism? There is plenty here, and more useful than mere ascetic exercises. If the walking on, in the sense of perpetual action-reaction-non-action in the course of each twenty-four hours, is truly ceaseless, you will get very tired, and your ego will be very rude to you, pleading and then screaming for indulgence. And you will be saying No. You may be feeling tired, ill, flat; you would rather be entertained or give yourself pleasure. This thing which should be done is inconvenient, too expensive in money, energy or time. If in spite of this you just go on with it because it seems the next right thing to be done, here is asceticism, and often more fierce than welcome!

Is it too limited? How can this be when the ideal act, whether great or small is performed, or should be, by the total man?

And the Goal? Does it matter at present? Enlightenment? I add to mine daily in carrying out what turns up to be done. I agree with H. P. Blavatsky: 'He who does not care for Heaven but is contented where he is, is already in Heaven'. Of course, at times one longs for 'the still centre of the turning world', which is Wordsworth's 'central peace, subsisting at the heart of endless agitation'. But where is it, if not here, and now, and doing this? Surely all action should be action in inaction, inaction in action, which is why non-action can be as powerful as any other form of it.

When a job comes our way, and seems ripe for the doing, let it then be done, 'in the scorn of consequence'. We *can* do no more; we *should* do no less. If done in love, in awareness of Life's totality, each act can be its own purpose, motive and reward.

Dharma-Yoga, then, can be an all-sufficient religion. If you wish, join it. Unceasingly find the Next-thing-to-be-done, and promptly and efficiently *do* it. You will find this a total and sufficient occupation for each hour of life, however spent, and suffused as you will be with joy and deep content, enormous fun!

IT HAS BEEN SAID

The immediate work, whatever it may be, has the abstract claim of duty, and its relative importance or non-importance is not to be considered at all.

H. P. Blavatsky

The selfish devotee lives to no purpose. The man who does not go through his appointed work in life—has lived in vain.

The Voice of the Silence

It is better to do one's own duty, even though devoid of excellence, than to perform another's duty well.

The Bhagavad Gita

WHAT DOES THE UNIVERSE WANT?

Our state of mind must be to want what the universe wants, in the way it wants it, in that place, at that time. This wanting *is* the Way.

R. H. Blyth

QUESTIONS

1 What to you are the ingredients of religion? Are they to be found in what you understand as Buddhism? Can Right Action become a religion sufficient for your purposes?

2 Are you in action all the time as suggested in Theme 5? If so, with what purpose and with what motive, to gratify the senses in what you call pleasure, or because you think that this thing is what you ought to do, that it is your duty?

3 Why do you so dislike the word duty? It only means what is due, what you owe. Is it because what you know you *ought* to do so frequently conflicts with what you *want* to do? If so, who wants so badly to avoid what another part of you knows to be due? The ego, self? Fie on you!

Theme 10
COMPASSION, UNIVERSAL LOVE

However we define love there are forms and degrees of it. At the lowest, friendliness for all, and some intensive love as a mother for her child. This can become involved in sexual desire, quite legitimately; it can diminish for many reasons or none, and it can become too fierce, amounting to a fault and not a virtue, as the intense possessive love which, as in some parent-child relationships, cripples and inhibits normal growth.

Higher is the love of head and heart combined, where the demand for regard or recognition, or at least insistence or the awareness of the beloved slowly dies, and it becomes increasingly impersonal.

LOVE WITHOUT ATTACHMENT

From the point of view of Zen we would say: 'Love the world and love the things of the world, all of them without exception, but do not love them for the pleasure they give you or hate them for the pain they bring you. That is to say, love them without attachment'.

R. H. Blyth in *Zen in English Literature*

JESUS ON LOVE

'Thou shalt love the Lord thy God with all thy heart, and with all thy soul, and with all thy mind.' This is the first and great commandment. And the second is like unto it, 'Thou shalt love thy neighbour as thyself'. On these two commandments hang all the Law and the prophets.

The Gospel according to St Matthew

Is not this magnificent and final? For God, read what you will of the Absolute, and for commandment, read a universal law.

If in fact Life is One, as set out in Theme 1 how can we still have enemies? Do the fingers of one hand hate one another?

Said Jesus, 'Ye have heard that it hath been said, "Thou shalt love thy neighbour, and hate thine enemy". But I say unto you, love your enemies, bless them that curse you, do good to them that hate you . . . ; that ye may be the children of your Father which art in heaven.'

This echoes a famous passage in the Buddhist scripture, the Dhammapada, containing, it is said, the Buddha's words of 500 years earlier. 'Hatred ceases not by hatred; hatred ceases but by love.' Try it!

At least consider the recent advice to the world given on television by the Dalai Lama, that instead of hating our enemies we should learn from them. For hate is a corrosive acid in the mind, and character is corroded by it. Perhaps this is why Buddhists set such store on the four 'Sublime States of Mind' and use them daily in meditation.

THE FOUR SUBLIME STATES OF MIND

I BENEVOLENCE

Here, with thoughts of benevolence, one pervades first one direction, then a second direction, then a third direction, then a fourth direction, then above, then below, then all around. Identifying oneself with all, one pervades the entire universe with thoughts of benevolence, with heart grown great, wide, deep, boundless, purified of all ill-will.

II COMPASSION

Here, with thoughts of compassion, one pervades first one direction, then a second direction, then a third direction, then a fourth direction, then above, then below, then all around. Identifying oneself with all, one pervades the entire universe with thoughts of compassion, with heart grown great, wide, deep, boundless, purified of all ill-will.

III   JOYOUS SYMPATHY

Here, with thoughts of joyous sympathy, one pervades first one direction, then a second direction, then a third direction, then a fourth direction, then above, then below, then all around. Identifying oneself with all, one pervades the entire universe with thoughts of joyous sympathy, with heart grown great, wide, deep, boundless, purified of all ill-will.

IV   EQUANIMITY

Here, with thoughts of equanimity, one pervades first one direction, then a second direction, then a third direction, then a fourth direction, then above, then below, then all around. Identifying oneself with all, one pervades the entire universe with thoughts of equanimity, with heart grown great, wide, deep, boundless, purified of all ill-will.

The love of man and woman at its best is a union of fellow pilgrims on this brief span of the long pilgrimage to Self-awareness. Some may find this Sermon a trifle ponderous, but is it not true?

THE ONE AND THE MANY

And there came to me a young man and a maiden in the springtime of their lives, shortly to be married, who, after courteous greetings, questioned me upon their new-found happiness. To whom I made reply: 'In the the beginning was the One which ever was and will be, being itself the womb of Time. From Unity was born Duality, as must be so when in the cycle of Eternity the Oneness is made manifest. From which in turn was born the Pairs of Opposites, two eyes within one head, within whose perfect focus lies the vision of their unity. As light to darkness, death to birth, each quality or being seeks its opposite, that in the Night of Sleep Duality may merge in One. In such a way Man-Woman came to being, dual-natured, as an undivided pair. But even as two nuts within a shell, on reaching earth the two-in-one was sundered. One emerged as two and in the darkness of the dawn the eyes of Woman met the eyes of Man and failed to see each other's complement. Since when, within the forest of

Samsara each has sought its lacking half, for union alone could heal their insufficiency. So shall it be until Avidya's shadows die before the Buddha Light and Woman-Man re-enters Unity.' The two before me seemed as though to speak. 'And we . . . who sought so long . . . have found . . . ?' 'Perfection's other half,' I smiling said, whose heart was warmed by such simplicity of love. 'Yet even as the One must manifest as Two, so from duality comes Three that from such trinity the Many may be born. Even as two were born of one so may the two perfect themselves as three, that Love, the binding force and product of the two, may symbolize their unity. Yet know that Love itself will one day have an end, for when the Many merge in One the Power which binds together all diversity will perish with its need. Yet, while Illusion lasts, let Love be as a lamp to guide your feet from spiritual darkness to the ways of Peace. Know that each seeming difference in point of view is as the outlook of two eyes within one head in whose united vision lies the Truth. Towards that Truth be steadfast in your journeying, until freed from the last of earth's entanglements, you enter hand in hand with all that lives that Silence which is Peace unutterable.'

And so they left me, wisdom in their eyes, and I, in all humility, was left to ponder on the beauty and the strength of Love.

From the meditations of Komo Ki

Compassion is a far higher faculty in the total man. This is indeed the Law of Laws, of which the Buddhist ideal, the Bodhisattva, 'he whose being is wisdom', is the ultimate expression. In that jewelled scripture, *The Voice of the Silence*, we learn much of this tremendous cosmic Force, perhaps the highest that the heart can ever know of the divine Light or Life of the Unborn.

But do not let thoughts of this mighty impersonal force of compassion lessen your sense of love for the beloved, your friends and all in need. Love, however we define the term, indeed 'makes the world go round', and a large number of those who in life 'go wrong' are found to have never known it in their childhood. It has been said that of love, health and money the most important is love. With it bad health may be endured, lack of money somehow surmounted.

Without it, what is the value of splendid health and a great deal of money? How miserable and lightless are those who know not love, or only in the violent form of desire to possess for themselves.

We must learn to control our emotion, and above all the least thought of hate, and its children, envy, jealousy and spite, for indeed they stain the mind as with corrosive acid. Love may be foolishly directed, uncomfortably expressed, but it is the light of the mind, the heart in triumph over thought, the solvent of grief and misery, our own and of those about us.

Let us then, while striving for the greater sense of awareness, divine compassion, still love on, wisely if we can, foolishly if we must, but ever in abundance. Read Rupert Brooke's long poem, 'The Great Lover', and learn to love just all about you. It is easy then to pass to people who need your love, if only to increase their own. There will be time enough to learn the meaning of impersonal compassion, boundless 'love in action' whence nothing is excluded, all included as one illumined, joyous Whole.

THE LAW OF LAWS

To some the Buddha is the All-Enlightened One—to others the All-Compassionate One. On these two wings, Enlightenment and pure Compassion, each one of us must rise. Of the pursuit of Wisdom much is to be found in Buddhist Scriptures; here let us consider what *The Voice of the Silence*, that jewelled fragment of the Golden Precepts, has to teach us on the nature of Compassion, and the need to practise it.

First let us savour to the full the following passage, for herein lies the key to many mysteries. 'Compassion is no attribute. It is the Law of laws, eternal Harmony, Alaya's Self; a shoreless universal essence, the light of everlasting Right, and fitness of all things, the law of love eternal.' Wherefore is it said, 'To live to benefit mankind is the first step,' and even to practise the six glorious virtues comes but second. Morality itself gives place to the dedication of one's inmost being to the needs of all mankind. To strive for self is to deny the Self, the garnered harvest of all our lives, and to delay its ultimate reunion with the SELF, that shoreless universal Essence which manifests as Life. Wherefore is it our bounden duty 'to step out from sunlight into shade, to make more room for others,' for with a growing realization of the law of Love we realize more and more that 'the selfish devotee lives to no purpose.'

Yet mere emotional goodwill is not compassion—we must seek it in the due performance of all duty. 'The man who does not go through his appointed work in life has lived in vain.' Learn to 'follow the wheel of life, follow the wheel of duty to race and kin, to friend and foe, and close thy mind to pleasures as to pain. Exhaust the law of Karmic retribution,' and so be free to know the SELF as ONE. Learn to eliminate the 'great dire heresy of separateness that weans thee from the rest,' for 'thou shalt not separate thy being from BEING, but merge the Ocean in the drop, the drop within the Ocean. So shalt thou be in full accord with all that lives; bear love to men as though they were thy brother pupils, disciples of one Teacher, the sons of one sweet mother,' until 'thou hast attuned thy heart and mind to the great heart and mind of all mankind.'

So shall the ultimate choice which waits us all be made each hour of the day, for 'the Path is one, Disciple, yet in the end, twofold. The first Path is Liberation, but the second is Renunciation, and therefore called the "Path of Woe".' Those who tread the second Path turn back on the threshold of Nirvana, unable to forget 'that mighty sea of sorrow formed of the tears of men'. To them in the silence of their own perfection comes a whisper from the heart of being—'Can there be bliss when all that lives must suffer? Shalt thou be saved and hear the whole world cry?' Wherefore let those who strive to follow in the footsteps of the All-Compassionate One read, and learn, and strive to realize the most exquisite expression of the Law yet given to man:

Let thy Soul lend its ear to every cry of pain like as the lotus bares its heart to drink the morning sun. Let not the fierce sun dry one tear of pain before thyself hast wiped it from the sufferer's eye. But let each burning human tear drop on thy heart and there remain, nor ever brush it off until the pain that caused it is removed.

BEYOND HAPPINESS

The price to be paid for this supernal level of love is high. Happiness, as we habitually use the term, will slowly fade out of consciousness. Surely the reason is obvious when we coldly and without emotion anyalse what this term means. It will be found to contain at least four ingredients, of which the first is a sense of security with a strong likelihood of the undisturbed continuance of the status quo. In the second place there must be an absence of worry, which to most men means an absence of that fruitful cause of worry, responsibility. Thirdly, there is an absence of strife or conflict, and fourthly, there is a powerful sense of comfort, involving a 'comfortable' income, good health, a happy home. Certain bolder spirits would allow occasional 'ups and downs' to add spice to life, and would claim to find time for a little mild philanthropy, but the mean conception approximates undoubtedly to the earthly idyll portrayed in myth and legend as the 'happy valley':

> Where falls not hail, or rain, or any snow,
> Nor ever wind blows loudly; but it lies
> Deep-meadow'd, happy, fair, with orchard-lawns
> And bowery hollows crowned with summer sea.

Such a conception is a lie, utterly selfish, and impossible of achievement. All manifestation is *anicca*, impermanent, *dukkha*, inseparable from suffering, and *anatta*, lacking a separate, unchanging self. The movement of life is a turning wheel, the Wheel of Rebirth, and happiness and unhappiness are but two of the 'pairs of opposites' which lie 'on either side of the circumference'. The flow of life itself is ever moving us on, and he who attempts to loiter on the highway will inevitably fall foul of a law which knows no argument. This constant movement involves suffering, in the sense of friction with other forms of life, a sense of dissatisfaction, of dis-ease. There are 'growing pains' of the mind as of the body, and the need of constant adjustment to countless ever-changing sets of circumstance involves a sense of strain which is itself a form of *dukkha*. Nor do we grow without making mistakes, and error is made known to us by commensurate pain. It follows that to cease suffering, in this sense, is to cease to grow, and life being movement, to stop is death. But the foolishness of seeking happiness is more apparent still to those who know the true nature of the self. Life has a million million forms, and not for a single instant has any one of them a monopoly of Self.

'There is no abiding principle in man,' no Spirit or Immortal Soul which is unchangingly and ultimately *his*. There is but One Life, and every form of it is but a temporary and partial manifestation of its Changelessness. It follows that the very self which seeks for happiness is itself unreal.

At least the Joy, which begins to shine as the more selfish love which is concealed in happiness departs, destroys the corrosive evil of hate.

LOVE AND HATE

And this I know, though men deny it every hour of the day, that Love is everything. Love, whether seen as Love or Hate, is ever binding men upon the Wheel; Love sets them free. Then what is Love? It would appear to be the one force that binds each separated fragment of Eternity to That from which it came. It welds the parts in one component Whole, the while its other aspect, Hate, would keep them free. From this it would appear that one day Hate will be reborn as Love, for Love and Hate are as the night and day, they alternate but cannot dwell together. Therefore, I say that not till Hate is all dissolved in Love will man be free to merge again into Reality. And thus I know, though men deny it every hour of the waking day, that Love, and Love alone, is everything.

From the meditations of Komo Ki

The understanding that Life is One now takes on a further meaning, and further reduces self and its minions, pride and envy, jealousy, and the fear that is destroyed by love. There is an exciting new sense that One is All and All is One, and a budding awareness of Totality. These following lines were written in the bombing of London in 1941.

I knew the bombing. I was there.
I felt the terror, saw the red blood spilled;
Heard thunder in the flame-lit air
And running feet that stumbled and were stilled.
I knew the bombing everywhere.
I watched the laws of love and hate fulfilled.
Of all the agony too wide aware
I suffered and was blinded and was killed.

I loved, and loving lived in hell,
I that am still unharmed, and well.

T. C. H.

There is a famous Buddhist Scripture which takes the ideal further still. Vimalakīrti is the personification of the layman who has attained enlightenment by his own efforts, comparable with that of the gods, and they all come to visit him when he is ill. Finally Mañjuśrī, the God of Wisdom, arrives with an enormous retinue, and they begin with a kind of Zen conversation:

'Mañjuśrī, you are welcome, Mañjuśrī, you are most welcome. You had not come and you come; you had not seen and you see; you had not heard and you hear.'

Mañjuśrī replies: 'It is indeed so, O householder, it is indeed as you say. He who has already come comes no more; he who has already left leaves no more. And why? Because he who has come no longer comes, he who has left no longer leaves, he who has seen no longer sees and he who has heard no longer hears.'

He continues by enquiring after Vimalakīrti's health, to which the latter responds:

'Mañjuśrī, my sickness will last while there lasts in beings ignorance and the thirst for existence. My sickness comes from afar, from the round of rebirth at its beginning. As long as beings are sick, I myself will also be sick; when beings recover, I also shall recover. And why? Mañjuśrī, for Bodhisattvas the realm of the round of rebirth is (made up of) beings, and sickness rests on this round of rebirth. When all beings have escaped the pains of this sickness, then Bodhisattvas also will be free of sickness.'

This exalted thought is reflected in the typical Bodhisattva Vow, never to enter Nirvana, however nobly earned, 'until the last blade of grass has entered in'.

But Compassion does not stand alone. Even as love is blind without some knowledge of how to help one's neighbour's need, so Wisdom and Compassion are the two sides of a coin, and even as Wisdom illumines Compassion, so Compassion, or in our human parlance love, are the hands of Wisdom acting with a thousand skilful devices to assist in the end of suffering and the reign of Joy.

The Wisdom referred to here, Prajna, is far beyond our human knowledge. Rather it is the vision or awareness when the intuition, 'a spark of the ultimate constituent of all things', 'the Oneness as the first-born of the Unborn', 'the highest spiritual power in our possession', as Dr Suzuki variously calls it, has illumined our knowledge and we *know* the right thing to do, how to express our love.

This Wisdom is its own authority; it is immediate, direct awareness of things as they are. In action, therefore, it is love incarnate, compassion ultimate. It has been said that Enlightenment turned inward is Wisdom, turned out is Compassion. And again, 'the Buddha enlightened himself by great Wisdom and saved all beings by his great Compassion'.

In the West, as already pointed out, we tend to live in the head, and the heart is gravely neglected. But is it not true that 'the head learns; the heart knows', and that they meet in skilful means for the helping of all life? The Lama Trungpa calls Compassion 'selfless warmth', and the Bodhisattva, however called or known, is its embodiment. A saying of Dr Suzuki's is most pertinent in the world today, that 'we can never save ourselves unless we save ourselves altogether, as a unit. Not just an individual, limited unity but the totality of individual units as a whole—then there comes the real compassion.'

All this must be applied, not merely quoted and discussed. And this as a habit of mind and heart in action every hour. There is no need to attempt to drop the self or ego if we truly love. There will be no room for it. Hence the grandeur and beauty of the Bodhisattva ideal. As we understand and reach its place we move into action, healing, helping, loving recklessly, unceasingly, and learning all the while. In the one interview between two very great men, Dr D. T. Suzuki and Father Merton, their recorded conversation ended with Dr Suzuki's words, after a moment's silence, 'the last word is love'.

THE BODHISATTVA

Waste not your praise on those now passionless.
In them the self is slow consumed in deeds
That flow responsive, eager, to the needs
Of man's totality. Such beings bless
All life by their own being. Here's no sense
Of sacrifice, no loss when fond belief
In severed self is minimal. No leaf
Upon the tree of life seeks recompense
From other, nor would loudly claim the sun
For personal possession. Deep at rest
In endless toil, life's weal their only quest,
These are content with duty gently done.
The mind the master of its thought; the sword
Of will the sheathèd power of the Void,
Here's human worth with gold of heaven alloyed

The Bodhisattva, careless of reward,
The incarnation of compassion, moves
With laughing eyes yet heart attuned to woe,
And with a thousand skilled devices proves
His inmost being's undivided flow,
A love so deep he knows not that he loves.

T. C. H.

IT HAS BEEN SAID

The desire and pursuit of the whole is called love.

Plato

To love universally is true humility.

From the Chinese

BOUNDLESS GOODWILL

Even as a mother, as long as she doth live, watches over her child, her only child,—even so should one practise an all-embracing mind unto all beings.

And let a man practise a boundless goodwill for all the world, above, below, across, in every way, goodwill unhampered, without ill-feeling or enmity.

The Pali Canon

Better you should be sullied by trying to help those in the mire than you should stand aloof and remain clean.

To feel 'compassion' without an adequate practical result ensuing from it is not to show oneself an 'altruist' but the reverse. Real self-development on the esoteric lines is *action*. 'Inaction in a deed of mercy becomes *an action* in a deadly sin'.

H. P. Blavatsky

He who will live for others shall have great troubles, but they will seem to him small. He who will live for himself shall have great troubles, but they will seem to him great.

Dean Inge

Love be in my head, and in my understanding.
Love be in my eyes and in my looking.
Love be in my mouth and in my speaking.
Love be in my heart and in my thinking.
Love be at mine end, and at my departing.

Traditional

QUESTIONS

1 Do you expect a return for your kindness and affection, if only by way of thanks? If so, this is surely a purchase, not a gift?

2 And has your willingness to help within the compass of your power a limit? If so, can it not be expanded?

3 'Hast thou attuned thy heart and mind to the great heart and mind of all humanity?'

The Voice of the Silence

THE APPROACH TO ENLIGHTENMENT

So far we have used faculties which all possess and consciously develop. But Truth needs the development of a new faculty, known in the West as the intuition.

It is important to understand clearly the profound distinction between the intellect and the intuition. This is not a form of super-thinking, and we must learn to admit that the intellect, however splendid in development, will never achieve the awareness, the direct fusion with Truth produced by the intuition.

Science, psychology, philosophy know a great deal about matter and the mind. They will never with the intellect alone *know* the truth concealed in these forms of study. They will never see what Buddhists call the Suchness, Is-ness, Be-ness of things in themselves. We must sooner or later learn to see things as they are, not as symbols or formulae of something else. As Dr Suzuki puts it, 'the intellect raises questions which it cannot answer' and never will, for the answer lies on a plane of consciousness beyond the reach of discriminating, pigeon-holing thought.

According to Eastern thought, Buddhi, the intuition, is the highest faculty in man. It is a lamp in every mind for the one Light waiting to be uncovered, realized, revealed. It provides an awareness of Totality beyond the Opposites, beyond the limitations of logic and what we conceitedly call good sense. It speaks in paradox. It must!

PARADOX

A paradox is not a kind of pun, to be explained by resolving the double meaning of the word. It does not spring from a desire to mystify one's hearers. It arises from the inability of language to say two things at once.

R. H. Blyth from *Zen in English Literature*

But just as there are degrees in the development of muscle, or thought-power, so the intuition, from rare and feeble 'peeps' will rise in time to full control and use. This 'mediumless perception' as it has been called, consists, says Dr Suzuki, of 'a system of intuitions' or, as he elsewhere calls it, grades of intuition from the most shallow to the deepest awareness. The deepest, he says, in his experience 'are those experienced by religio-philosophical minds belonging to the order of the Prajaparamita ("the Wisdom that has gone Beyond"). But when their intuitions are translated into terms of relative knowledge, how insipid, negative and nonsensical'. From this fact comes the challenging but profound statement that nothing we say is ever or ever can be true; it is only partial. Nothing has yet been said since the world began which was True! Because words are concepts and symbols, and Truth is awareness before the first concept, with its limitations of duality, was born. Carl Jung says the same in his own words.

WHEN SPIRIT DECLINES TO INTELLECT

Only after the decline of the Middle Ages, when spirit began to degenerate into intellect, there set in a reaction against the unbearable domination of intellectualism which led to the pardonable mistake of confusing intellect with spirit, and blaming the latter for the misdeeds of the former. Intellect does in fact violate the soul when it tries to possess itself of the heritage of the spirit. It is in no way fitted to do this because spirit is something higher than intellect in that it includes not only the latter, but the feelings as well.

From *The Secret of the Golden Flower*

Note the important relationship here emphasized. Those who strive to develop the intuition do not thereby show contempt for the intellect or feelings, but from the higher standpoint assess them at their true worth and use them wisely in the field to which they belong.

All this is the foundation of a large distinction recently emphasized by several minds. In the Middle Ages man had a soul in relation to a God, but the God was outside him. When the decline from spirit to intellect mentioned above began to produce a void of spirit, the advanced minds among men began to look *within* for a God whose innate fusion with all manifested things removed the

134

duality implied in any search for the Mind or Self or true soul of man.

It is interesting to note the distinction between intuitive Wisdom and intellectual knowledge in those scriptures recognized as of timeless value in the wide field of religion. Each was born of the spiritual awareness/experience of the writer, whoever he was, and can be distinguished sharply from the often dreary commentaries at intellectual level which surround them, and too often veil their light. Why do all religious aspirants revere those scriptures? I claim that enough for a lifetime's use can be placed on a bookshelf in the space of twelve inches, and each book would go in the pocket or bag. Such works as the *Bhagavad Gita*, the *Tao Te Ching*, the Fourth Gospel, the *Sutra of Hui Neng*, the *Dhammapada*, *The Voice of the Silence*, all these speak from the plane beyond the reach of thought-created prose. They speak, so far as words can enable them, out of Reality, an intuitive, immediate awareness of the truths therein enshrined.

But as the intuition develops there is an intermediate stage, it is suggested, between thought at high level and intuitive awareness, that which I have called Illumined Thought. It is as though the whole workshop of high thinking were raised up to the steady Light of Buddhi which brilliantly illumines our awareness as we consciously and, so far as possible, persistently lift consciousness towards it. After all, in order to read small print we lift the book as near as possible to the lamp, and the same may apply to the advancement of our understanding, our direct understanding of what we want to know.

One way or another, having recognized the existence of the intuition as the sole source of any direct awareness of Reality, we shall get 'peeps', sudden is the operative word, in 'moments of no time', when a feeling/thought suddenly flames with certainty, and we vainly try to explain to those about us, in the home or circle of friends, just what we have now 'seen'. But you cannot describe this new awareness, for words are below the plane on which it lives. Here is the birth of what the Japanese Zen Buddhists call *Satori*.

There are those who know the anguished ecstasy which an artist, musician, or poet feels when the mood of inspiration is upon him; there are those who share the amazed delight of the philosopher when a further glimpse of Reality lights up his consciousness; many

135

have known how a young man or maid in love re-views the whole of life, yet none of these achieve the unearthly joy which comes to the Zen practitioner as the reward of patient, unremitting toil. Here is a vision which 'maketh all things new,' a fundamental change in one's point of view. Until the moment when *Satori* is first experienced, the world around is seen from the circumference, from the standpoint of oneself; henceforth one sees it from the centre of the circle, from the standpoint of the All. Until this moment one views Reality from one's place upon the Wheel; when the vision breaks, the realm of the Unchanging is seen for what it is, and worldly life as the moon reflected in water, as a pale reflection of the Light that glows within. Here is no false emotion, no mere 'psychic experience,' for though the vision fades as we prove too feeble to hold our consciousness at such exalted levels, yet its memory remains and every time the vision is seen it lasts a little longer and has more power to influence our lives. Whether it comes in meditation or at seemingly irrelevant moments in the day, its force is cumulative as a power for good, for it is a foretaste of a state of consciousness that one day will be normal for each one of us.

How, then, is *Satori* to be attained? The answer is by years and lives of hard, consistent effort. The chief obstacle in this development is the intellect, and no progress will be made until the essential difference between intuitive and intellectual knowledge is clearly understood. To *know* is as distinct from to *think* as 'to think' is distinct from 'to feel with the emotions'. Hence the apparent irrelevance of the times and places of *Satori* and of the curious methods used by Zen Masters to break the bonds of intellectual reasoning. With the birth of this inner vision, however, comes such a change of spiritual values, such a re-creation of the Universe and our essential part in it, that all the toil and effort is known to be well worth the ineffable reward.

Each sudden peep is personal, yet impersonal. It is, it has been said, incommunicable, unmistakable and unforgettable. It may come after long thought but it is not, and one must press this point again, the result of thinking, however high.

Its impersonality is important to accept. There is vision; none sees or is now aware. And we cannot command it. As Aldous Huxley pointed out in his *Adonis and the Alphabet*. 'We cannot make ourselves understand; the most we can do is to foster a state of mind in which understanding may come to us.'

This new awareness is Wisdom beyond knowledge, Beauty beyond its forms, Truth beyond the Opposites, indeed before they were born. So is Joy far beyond happiness.

JOY AND SORROW

Weeping may endure for a night, but joy cometh in the morning.
(Psalm 30.5)

Sorrow and happiness are opposites. Both are in a state of perpetual change; both circle round the self. Joy is different. Joy is a quality of raised consciousness, of a mind illumined by the intuition. Once achieved, and to the extent habitually held, it is a 'higher third' above all pairs of opposites. As Beauty transcends prettiness and ugliness; as Compassion is above both love and hate; as Truth is above the true and false, so Joy is above the changing accidents of happiness/unhappiness and pleasure/pain. In Joy one is not of course oblivious to the physical and mental conditions of daily life. One is still well or ill, emotionally at peace or in deep distress, mentally content or clouded with illusion. But these alternatives, under the power of Joy are accepted, digested and largely ignored. I *have* a toothache, a relation dying, my job in peril; I *am* to be married, have found a home, have won a large sum on a horse race.

So what? as one may ask in modern terms. Do all these happenings affect my inner Joy? There are those who answer No, so let us consider what this power may be. It is clearly not born in the world of Samsara, of duality, of 'the lower mind'. It is as clearly a quality beyond the limits of thought, of the Wisdom which Dr Suzuki calls Prajna-intuition. It may be achieved in 'moments', 'peeps' of new awareness, or help to illumine a mind which now knows just a little of Wisdom, Compassion, Truth and Beauty on their own supernal plane.

At least it is worth our striving, our determination to 'see' that behind the clouds of suffering and grief, of hatred, lust and illusion,

Joy is already shining. Truly 'weeping may endure for a night, but joy cometh in the morning'.

Santana

As the self-made fetters of thinking/feeling fall, the mind begins to waken to the great truth, 'Waken the mind to abide nowhere'. As the self's loud voice is less heard, the soft virtue of humility has more chance to appear. And there is new meaning in the equally great saying, 'There are no others'.

LIVING FOR OTHERS

Look, I pray, in thought and feeling away from these external problems which you have written down in your letter; draw on the breath of the great life throbbing in us all and let faith (which is unlearned knowledge) carry you through your life as a bird flies through the air—undoubtingly. Only remember one thing—when once you fling yourself on the great life of Nature, the force that keeps the world in motion and our pulses beating and which has within it, in its heart, a supreme and awful power—once having done that, you can never again claim back your life. You must let yourself swing with the motion of the spheres. You must live for other men and with them; not for or with yourself.

From a Master's letter to W. Q. Judge

And many a false distinction begins to disappear.

MOUNTAINS AND TREES

To those who know nothing of Zen, it is said, mountains are just mountains, trees are just trees, and men are just men. After one has studied Zen a little, mountains are no longer mountains, trees are no longer trees and men are no longer men. But to him who fully understands Zen, mountains are once again mountains, trees are once again trees, men are once again men. In other words, the objective world has to die a kind of death, that it may be resurrected in its true body. The old world, so stale beneath the incrustation of habit, is destroyed as an illusion, but, with

Enlightenment, a new one comes into being; nothing has been lost yet all is changed.

Gai Eaton

There is a new-found glory and joy in all about us. As a Zen master would say, 'Every day is a good day' if we can but see it so. Browning was right.

HEAVEN AND EARTH

> There shall never be one lost good. What was, shall live as before;
>> The evil is null, is nought, is silence implying sound;
> What was good shall be good, with, for evil, so much good more;
>> On the earth the broken arcs; in the heaven, a perfect round.
> All we have willed or hoped or dreamed of good, shall exist;
>> Not its semblance but itself; no beauty, nor good nor power
> Whose voice has gone forth, but each survives for the melodist
>> When eternity affirms the conception of an hour.
> The high that proved too high, the heroic for earth too hard,
>> The passion that left the ground to lose itself in the sky,
> Are music sent up to God by the lover and the bard;
>> Enough that He heard it once; we shall hear it by and by.

From 'Abt Vogler'

So far the musician. The same applies, as the Light suffuses our noblest thinking, to the student of the Wisdom, and to all compassionate workers for mankind.

Old opposites begin to fuse in one, especially self and Self, as the self becomes more and more the machine of the personality newly cleaned and controlled.

THE SELF IS THE PERSONALITY

But we must distinguish carefully the self or ego and the personality, the former as a compound of animal instincts which should have been outgrown and the illusion that there can be such a thing as separate existence; the latter as a set of clothes or vehicles or powers of the man we know, whether we know him at the moment as a great man or a small man, lovable or unlovable, with his name and address, his home and job and special attributes.

The Self, which we are now learning consciously to be on more occasions and for longer hours, dominates the self, or should, as a dog brought to heel, and uses the latter wisely as he needs, to express himself at his best in the world of man.

BRIGHTON PIER

Lean over Brighton Pier. Observe the waves that rise and fall (no more) and each the product of its neighbour. Observe on this one suddenly a spume of blue-white water, dancing, for a space of moments, on the undivided sea. It has shaped form, and size and colour, and beauty of its own. It dies, dissolves, its wetness, blue-and-whiteness, all that made it so, returned, all purpose spent, to mother-ocean.

What made it so, what blend of moon-led tide and ocean-thrust and vagrant, windy sky forged once, with fused uncertainty of power, that sunlit wavelet on a dancing sea?

And I that lean, and pondering observe, what provenance have I? A million moments, seed of other millions, were, and being so just this am I.

But who is this that speaks of this, who watches both observer and the sea? He knows the wavelet of his name and form; content and happily diffused, he knows himself no thing but Ocean. Whence the sea?

It is no matter; in the mind set free there is no-wavelet dancing on no-sea! No Self to tell no self it shall not be! Only the dancing pier, the happy wave, and me!

Santana

We are climbing, lifting consciousness above the level on which we fought and wrangled, and loudly expressed ourselves as worthy of attention. The Self, ourselves at our best, now lives more in the Eternal, seeing the field of Samsara as the field of experience in which to work out Dharma, duty, 'the next thing to be done'. In our raised consciousness, to change the metaphor, we are moving towards the Centre. Prajna/Karuna, Wisdom and Compassion, are seen as covering the ambit of our newly seen part in the Plan of the Universe which is our job to be done. Let us seek this Centre.

In it we shall find the Suchness of things, and see things as they
ARE.

IT HAS BEEN SAID

One of the two sought long and painfully for the great solution.
One day, when he was weeping bitterly, he suddenly regarded his
companion through his tears and said, 'So it's you!'

Hasidic story

All beauty, all music, all poetry is a dancing of the mind. Without
this dancing of the spirit there is no true Zen.

R. H. Blyth

All the shadows in the Universe cannot put out the light of one
candle.

To see into where there is no 'something', that is the true seeing.

Foolish are they who turn their backs on the light and argue about
the nature of the shadow in front.

There is nothing infinite apart from finite things.

D. T. Suzuki

QUESTIONS

1 Do you now clearly see the difference between knowing about and
knowing, an intellectual understanding capable of proof or
disproof, addition, modification and argument—and knowing not
only beyond argument, but beyond description of what one
knows?

2 Do you find new meaning in the puzzling phrase in *The Voice of
the Silence*, that 'Mind is the slayer of the Real'?

3 Can you at least conceive of a beyond of duality or, better still, a
condition before the dualism, which Dr Suzuki loves to call the
bifurcation, occurred? At least do you genuinely see, whatever
your education and mind-training, that the intellect alone can
never KNOW? And the need of a faculty which can?

Theme 12
ENLIGHTENMENT

We shall not know full Enlightenment. Not even the Buddha, whose mind it is said 'could rove the interstellar spaces while yet retaining full consciousness under the Bo Tree', had reached the end of it. For the totality of it is and must be Totality itself, the return of manifestation to the silence of the Absolute. But we shall approach just that much nearer, even a foot or two, in the application of this Course. Let us therefore speak of the approach to enlightenment, noting the meaning of the word as itself a process of becoming enlightened. Let us pause humbly if we seem to have lifted consciousness to some small awareness of what in our imagining we believe it to be. For, as already set out in Theme 11, there are degrees and grades of enlightenment, and the hundred names for it may be so many labels for mere degrees of it. None of us can measure another's awareness. Our own mystics of all ages speak of it with every superlative available. For the moment it is enough for us to know that it is the end of the limitations caused by the sense of 'I'. Let us face it. It is indeed sui-cide, self-murder, and we must take it on faith from those far ahead of us on the Way that in this death is a life so wide, so filled with Light and its expression, love, that self is well dead and finally cremated!

Even a first taste of it will enable us to understand the now famous phrase of Father Merton's, though others of course have made this clear since the dawn of language.

ZEN INSIGHT

Zen insight is not *our* awareness, but Being's awareness of itself in us. This is not a loss of self in 'nature' or 'the One'; it is not a withdrawal to one's spiritual essence and a denial of matter and the world. On the contrary, it is recognition that the whole world is aware of itself in me, and that 'I' am no longer my individual and limited self, still less a disembodied soul, but that my 'identity' is to be sought not in that

143

separation from all that is, but in oneness with all that is. This identity is not the denial of my own personal reality but its highest affirmation. It is a discovery of *genuine identity* in and with the One. . . .

Thomas Merton in *Thomas Merton on Zen*

'Being's awareness of itself in us'. Here is religion at its highest, the true surrender of what we are not into the arms of what we are. Here is obedience to the 'Power divine' described in *The Light of Asia*, and the explanation of the oft derided phrases of Christian mystics when they speak of return to the Beloved.

Indeed, as Gai Eaton writes, 'Every actual experience is a little death, the extinction of self-consciousness', and the corresponding awakening of Being's consciousness in us.

The most famous and the most violently direct way to the experience is that obtaining still today, after 1500 years, in the Rinzai Zen school of Japanese Buddhism. It is of course extremely difficult. It needs tremendous strength of purpose and total dedication. It is therefore and always has been for the few, and this is no place for a thesis on Zen Buddhism.

But the word Zen having been mentioned, please note a profound and important distinction, between the Ultimate, Absolute, Nameless Totality, and our limited conception of it. George Calery has made the point well in the case of that deep experience known in Zen Buddhism as *Satori*.

TWO KINDS OF ZEN

There are two kinds of Zen. The first is capital ZEN, the *experience* of the unattainable cosmic consciousness, *Satori*, enlightenment, wholeness or whatever name gets analogously applied. That experience is out of the range of language or intellection. It cannot be killed no matter what labels one applies. It cannot be limited or extended by definition. The other is lower-case Zen; the rich, vitally alive tradition which carried expressions of the above realization, practicable methods and commentaries, and serves as a means to that realization. This Zen is totally within the realm of language. ZEN is always the goal; Zen a vehicle, method or path to that goal. Zen is a vitally alive tradition to the extent that it serves ZEN.

From *The Middle Way*, November 1975

But to reach ZEN we must rise through the lower levels of consciousness and achieve some understanding of Zen, or its equivalent in some other name.

PROGRESS

There's pleasure in the body, strange delight
In all the functions of the day and night.
The lust of warmth, the belly's deep content;
The feel of fur, and sleep's abandonment.
The smell of wine, of woman's hair,
A bonfire, heavy on the autumn air;
But lust of heart is better.

The feel of fear, resolved in swift relief;
Blind anger, brutal past belief
To reason kneeling, and heart's kindliness
That fills the throat and runs to bless
The littlest form of life; and jealousy,
Conceived of love, whatever that may be;
Yet lust of thought is better.

Mind, the unswerving searchlight of the soul,
Womb and destroyer of each partial whole.
To build with cold, conceptual glee
The shrine of an ideal, then set it free,
And nobler build, moving on Godlike feet
Towards the vision of the thing complete;

But give me Zen.

T. C. H.

But Enlightenment is no prerogative of Zen Buddhism. What is it? It is said that even the least experience of it is incommunicable, unmistakable and unforgettable. In the 'scriptures' of Zen Buddhism, meaning the recorded sayings of Zen masters, there is

145

much talk of the Gradual and the Sudden School. But the difference has no permanent validity. True, the experience comes suddenly, without warning, without apparent cause, but the development of the inner faculties which led to it were indeed gradual, step by step, over probably many lives of effort to the same indescribable end.

There will, of course, be what a student in a Zen Class called 'pop-outs', or more politely, 'peeps'. These are small but genuine 'moments of no time' when the intuition flashed its message to the wakening mind. They must not be confused with psychic hunches, though the identification may not for a while be easy. Psychic hunches come from the psychic or astral plane, one above the physical in our analysis in Theme 2. The flash of the new awareness is born of the will.

> Enlightenment must involve the will as well as the intellect. It is an act of intuition born of the will.
>
> D. T. Suzuki

English poets have written of this experience.

> Last night I lay in an open field
> And looked at the stars with lips sealed;
> No noise moved the windless air,
> And I looked at the stars with steady stare.

> But through a sudden gate there stole
> The Universe, and spread in my soul;
> Quick went my breath and quick my heart,
> And I looked at the stars with lips apart.
>
> From J. C. Squire's 'Starlight'.

The life of Zen begins with the opening of *Satori*, which may be defined as an intuitive looking into the nature of things in contradistinction to the analytical or logical understanding of it.

> D. T. Suzuki

THROUGH-WAY

This bright awareness of un-common sense
Is sudden Zen. But now, walk on, my friend.
The fool will pause at such experience,
But here's a true beginning, not the end.

Mu-shin

Are you still trying to think it? Think again. Truth cannot be the product of thought, but this very thought is difficult to drive into the mind. A thought or concept involves memory, imagination (image-making) projection into a world which is built on duality. It *is* this, *not* that, and so on. The intuition KNOWS, even thought it lacks the built-up machinery of logical thinking to create the experience down at the level of a thought. Try the following. It's true!

THE VOID

The Void is filled
With forms of emptiness
And things which are not there.

Omai

This doctrine of the Void, in Sanskrit, *Sunya-ta* Empti-ness, is the highest metaphysics achieved by man, but it is not for us here, although it was mentioned in Theme One.

But we, meanwhile, deliberately moving towards a conceived purpose, this actual experience of what we will here call *Satori*, are in Duality. *Satori* is not so much beyond the least touch of duality as on that level of consciousness before the One became Two, 'pre-bifurcation' as Dr Suzuki loved to call it.

AWAKING

Enlightenment is not a mere personal affair which does not concern the community at large; its background is laid in the universe itself. . . . That *I* have been able to conceive a great longing for enlightenment means that the entire world wishes to be liberated from ignorance and evil passions. . . . It requires a long preparation, not of one life but of many lives. . . . The great ocean of transmigration drowns everybody that goes into it. Especially the philosophers, who are satisfied with interpretations and not with facts themselves, are utterly unable to extricate themselves from the bondage of birth and death, because they never cut asunder the invisible tie of Karma and knowledge that securely keeps them down to the earth of dualities because of their intellectualism. Therefore the awakening . . . which takes place in the depths of one's being is a great religious event.

D. T. Suzuki

And this great event is not merely to see that each of the opposites is a mode of the other, but that both came from and are two simultaneously identical expressions of the same thing!

The most famous poem in Zen Buddhism was composed by the Patriarch Seng-t 'San (died A.D. 606).

STANZAS FROM 'ON TRUST IN THE HEART'

2 To set up what you like against what you dislike
  That is the disease of the mind.
  When the deep meaning of the Way is not understood
  Peace of mind is disturbed to no purpose.

10 Abide not with dualism;
   Carefully avoid pursuing it;
   As soon as you have right and wrong
   Confusion ensues and Mind is lost.

25 In the higher realms of true Suchness
   There is neither 'self' nor 'other'.
   When direct identification is sought
   We can only say 'not two'.

30 One in All;
   All in One—
   If only this were realized
   No more worry about your not being perfect!

31 When Mind and each believing mind are not divided
   And undivided are each believing mind and Mind,

This is where words fail;
For it is not of the past, present and future.

tr. by D. T. Suzuki

All Zen masters, and many of the great minds in the history of world thought, accept this basis concept of Not-Two (which is higher than One for it is not One either!). It is the denial of all duality and of the existence of any two (separate) things in existence. They are each some part of the One which yet is all of the '10,000 things', as the Chinese call Samsara. It is utterly basic to all thinking about Enlightenment and the experience achieved in Enlightenment. It means precisely what it says, that there are no two things in existence separate from one another though to our eyes and minds and to our own consciousness they seem so. This is 'the still centre of the turning world', the centre of 'the circle whose circumference is nowhere'. It is 'the centre in the midst of conditions' referred to in *The Secret of the Golden Flower*, and it is unshakeable in its equanimity. When achieved there is, as already said a dozen times herein, no self to know it. Here is the goal of religion beyond the forms or indeed the need of it. As Wordsworth wrote, no person visits or becomes one with any Person. He is in that moment,

Rapt in the still communion that transcends
The imperfect offices of prayer and praise.

In that moment or even somewhere near it, one may live as the Bhagavad Gita puts it, in 'a constant and unswerving steadiness of heart to every event, whether favourable or unfavourable'. It is well worth trying to raise the level of habitual consciousness just so much nearer that ideal.

Yet beware of a smug, self-praising attitude of indifference to all events. We are part of them all, being ourselves the All, and we must remember to laugh, at everything, ourselves never for one moment excluded.

LIGHTNESS OF SPIRIT

Zen most clearly exemplifies the quality of lightness inherent in Spirit. Weight belongs to the earth, and it is earthly matters that are grim and earnest, steeped in the perpetual anxiety which every morality has recognized as the root of sin.

Gai Eaton

We are on the Way. We are indeed all 'on the Way', but perhaps a few more have now made the self-dedication, the Self-dedication, to tread it at whatever cost to all that in our hazy and ill-lit mind we call dear. If so, we are committed to an end we know not, filling our minds with ever more Wisdom and our hearts with ever-increasing Love.

ONWARD

The falling tide of darkness flows away.
    The voice of self is stilled.
I am a child with opened eyes of day,
    A vessel yet unfilled.

I am alone yet seek not any friend.
    I feel the heart of woe.
The face is veiled of my appointed end,
    Yet this I know.

The future lies unmoulded in my hands.
    A Path winds out before.
There is no backward way. Behind me stands
    A closèd door.

T. C. H.

NIRVANA

You still want to know about Nirvana? None can speak of its nature for it has none. Perhaps Sir Edwin Arnold said as much as may be said.

If any teach Nirvana is to cease,
    Say unto such they lie.
If any teach Nirvana is to live,
    Say unto such they err . . .
The Light of Asia

The famous monk, Nagasena put it more pithily still when expounding basic Buddhism to the Greek Emperor Menanda: 'Nirvana IS'.

We need no formulated purpose now. We are losing all desire even for Nirvana!

Nirvana is not for those who desire it, for Nirvana is the absence of desire.

To achieve this 'non-awareness' Zen Buddhists work on a *koan*, the Zen term for a phrase or word which has no meaning making sense to the intellect. Try one if you will, but do not burst the brain in trying to 'think out' the unthinkable.

Draw a line from North to South and there is neither East nor West.

I wept into the sea. It did not overflow.

The hill goes up and down.

IT HAS BEEN SAID

Total awareness is a primary, choiceless, impartial response to the present situation as a whole.

Aldous Huxley

'I' can never become enlightened.

Muriel Pugh

We shall never be more in Eternity than we are now.

The aim of Zen is to restore the experience of original inseparability.

After all, strength is in visioning the empty.

Nothing is better than anything good.

The truth of Zen is the truth of life, and life means to live, to move, to act, not merely to reflect. . . . When I raise the hand thus, there is Zen. But when I assert that I have raised the hand, Zen is no more there.

D. T. Suzuki

QUESTIONS

1 You have taken this Course. Why? To obtain what? What have you got?

2 What are you willing to surrender, to pay for what you got?

3 To the extent that you have failed, what has been resisting your efforts to get what you wanted?

4 What are you doing all day, every day to overcome this resistance or in some way cope with it?

5 Why?

INSTEAD OF CONCLUSION

So much for the Course, itself the product of long years of Class work with fellow seekers, old and young, of East and West, but all in search of Self, the One Self to be found within.

What you have got out of it will be in strict proportion to what you put into it, of time and energy and intelligent use all day.

In the end, all turns, have you not found, on Application? Study and Meditation, and other forms of digestion, are but preparation for constant Application of spiritual force to the somewhat low grade mixture of vice and virtue of which our life in society is composed. At the end of each day try asking yourselves, 'What have I done, learnt, understood, become, today more than was true last night? Where now is my habitual level of consciousness? Just that much higher than it was before, just so much nearer the level of the Self? Or, as someone put it, less in the gutter and more in the sky?'

How do we slowly reach that higher level? How, save by habit, a newly formed habit, of heart and mind and body? The rest will follow as the night the day. And this new habit is largely a change in comparative values. Which now matters *more* to you, the daily round, which is of course a perfectly legitimate occupation, or the Search carried on in the course of it? If we are not yet the Self, which is the flame of the Light, are we more and more living 'as if' we were, and so producing a fusion of the unreal and the Real? A fusion of the ego which is definitely not Self and the Self which is? Are we just so much nearer to possessing and exhibiting what Gerald Gould so exquisitely called

> 'a careless trust
> In the divine occasion of our dust'?

If so we must teach, all of us. This is a solemn and somewhat frightening thought, filled with new effects and danger and responsibility. But surely all who have, however dimly, seen the Way to which the finger points, must do the same for those who are but other Selves, although there are, as we shall by now have learnt, 'no others'?

153

The Voice of the Silence is clear enough on the subject of our duty.

Point out the Way, however dimly, and lost among the host, as does the evening star to those who tread their path in darkness.

Give light and comfort to the toiling pilgrim, and seek out him who knows still less than thou; who in his wretched desolation sits starving for the bread of Wisdom, without a Teacher, hope or consolation, and—let him hear the Law.

At least we can attempt to teach the first principles of truth and right conduct as the Course has helped us find.

'GO YE FORTH, O BHIKKHUS'

Go ye forth, brethren, for the profit of the many, for the bliss of the many, out of compassion for the world, for the welfare, the profit, the bliss of *devas* and mankind!

Go not any two together. Proclaim, brethren, the Dhamma, goodly in its beginning, goodly in its middle, goodly in its ending. Both in the spirit and in the letter do ye make known the all-perfected, utterly pure righteous life. There are beings with but little dust of passion on their eyes. They are perishing through not hearing the Dhamma. There will be some who will understand.

From the Pali Canon

A guide, on finding a man who has lost his way, brings him back to the right path. He does not jeer at him. You must show the unlearned man the truth, and you will see that he will follow. But so long as you do not show it him, you should not mock, but rather feel your own incapacity.

Source unknown

But face that the responsibility for any attempt to transmit a spiritual truth is great. If this be true of the teaching of the making and use of high explosives in a laboratory, it is far truer of the cosmic force contained in a spiritual principle. If the pupil abuses the power which your teaching gives him, yours is the Karma of his wrong use of it. Hence the long list in religious history of tests, examinations 'initiations', in the sense of a careful handing over to the pupil now

154

ready to use wisely what is revealed. True, in a sense one only teaches a pupil to find truth for himself. Thus the Buddha taught. 'Even Buddhas do but point the way.' But he gave much detail of each footstep on the Way.

Even the simplest meditation, as we have seen, produces power which with evil motive will have grave results. Teach what? Someone gave his own brief summary. Have you found these to be true?

IN BRIEF

Truth is unbelievably simple. Its complexity is falsely imagined, and of our own creation. It is we who create an intellectual fog of distinctions, definitions, comparisons, rival doctrines and exclusive forms. Only the intuition, seeing the thing as it is, suddenly knows and is amused at the previous fog. Try these Propositions.

1 The Purpose of it all is Enlightenment, an awareness, slowly becoming permanent, that every part is the Whole, meaning no less than the WHOLE.

2 Therefore all sense of separation, of the part's rights against the Whole, is also falsely imagined.

3 Therefore the ego can never succeed as such for more than a brief period of time, any more than a swimmer can indefinitely swim upstream.

4 All attempts to maintain a separate identity breed suffering, both for the holder of the belief and thence for all mankind.

5 Therefore, to reduce all suffering reduce the sense of self-importance, desire for self-gratification, and belief in the reality of a separate self.

6 To this end allow a sense of Wholeness to expand within. Allow the total Buddha-Mind to suffuse all thought, purpose and action, leaving less and less room, time and energy for ego. Walk on!

Santana

But we must not be afraid to drop a hint or two to someone who seems to be in need of what we at least believe we know. We all have something to share.

No one has the right to remain idle on the excuse that he knows too little to teach. For he may always be sure that he will find others who know still less than himself. It is not until a man begins to try to teach others that he discovers his own ignorance and tries to remove it.

H. P. Blavatsky

But give good thought to what you teach, and to whom and how. It should not lightly be dogmatic doctrine which you yourself may later find to be untrue. It should be what you *know* to be true.

Truth repeated is no longer truth; it becomes truth again only when it has been realized by the speaker as an immediate experience.

Aldous Huxley

For that which comes in actual experience is something of which you may truly say, 'Thus have I found'.

It is, however, desperately hard to keep a middle Way between the extremes of interference and neglect. The Bhagavad Gita is clear enough—'There is danger in another's duty'. So is *The Voice of the Silence* to the opposite effect. 'Inaction in a deed of mercy is an action in a deadly sin.'

Each in the end must tread the way of his own choosing and learn from his own errors, just as children must be allowed to hurt themselves in order to learn the wisdom of the advice given them.

Prepare thyself, for thou wilt have to travel on alone. The Teacher can but point the Way. The Path is one for all; the means to reach the goal must vary with the pilgrims.

The Voice of the Silence

Be humble as you pass on the Wisdom you have gained. The Teaching is not yours, and the less 'you' come into it the better. The ideal analogy is that of the conduit pipe, the impersonal instrument or means for letting the Wisdom, ever-present, flow into the now receptive mind.

Self-watchfulness is never more necessary than when a personal wish to lead, and wounded vanity, dress themselves in the peacock's feathers of devotion and altruistic work.

H. P. B.

How shall we recognize a teacher qualified and 'right' to teach us? 'Beware of Guru-hunting', we were told long ago. There are always many only too ready to fall at the feet, almost literally nowadays, of anyone with impressive claims to make certain their success in the Search. But if these claimants have this power why are they not themselves visibly, enormously enlightened? If books and our meditation and practical experience will not help us fast enough, use, for that is the right word, the help of someone who will help. But remember the immortal phrase,

> 'When the pupil is ready the master appears'. 'We need a man who can master our hearts; for this is the essential quality of true teaching, that it raises echoes in the depths of our being, resonances we recognize because they sound the notes of truly human aspiration.'

Sri Madhava Ashish in Man, Son of Man

Such a man will teach from where he is to the pupil where he is, not from a lordly tower of dogmatism.

> 'You can only help a man from his own level'.

Presumably this famous saying means that we can only help another by rousing or helping him to uncover the one Light already within him.

> 'It is more profitable to kindle an inspiration than to win a conviction'.

Here is a lovely story of this:

> Two men were discussing bitterly. A child passed by saying: 'See what a lovely flower I have found'. The two men looked at him, and when he had passed, each said to the other: 'Well, I think you are right'.

And in our form of teaching the suggested truth or book to read, it is wise to be 'with it', to flow with current similes and trend of thought.

Those who study the traditional doctrines must keep in mind the Buddhist saying that, 'Whatever is not adapted to such and such persons as are to be taught cannot be called a teaching'; remaining sensitive to the currents of thought and prevailing tendencies of their time, they must be prepared, as far as they are able, to translate the universal truths into terms that correspond to the Western mind and character as they find it, without, in the process adulterating them'.

Gai Eaton in The Richest Vein

There seem to be two levels of teaching

1 By precept and quotation: 'Thus have I heard . . .' This is Wisdom, knowledge digested, but not necessarily by the speaker.
2 By example:
No man can help his fellow save by the force of his example, save by the spectacle of his achieved holiness.

From Myers' The Root and the Flower

What you are speaks so loudly that I cannot hear what you say.

Emerson

Let your light so shine before men that they may see your good works and glorify your Father which is in Heaven.

Gospel according to St Matthew

But however we teach the following is true:

Knowledge increases in proportion to its *use*, that is, the more we teach the more we learn.

H. P. Blavatsky

NOT TWO

But all this discussion of teacher and pupil is false. Is it not true, and well said, that:

No teacher has more than one pupil, himself.
No pupil has more than one teacher, himself.

Walk on, for now you must!

SHORT BIBLIOGRAPHY
of books quoted or found to be helpful

SCRIPTURES AND COMMENTARIES

The Bhagavad Gita.

The Dhammapada, ed. Radhakrishnan. O.U.P. 1950.

The Gospel According to St John.

The Sutra of Hui Neng, tr. Wong Mou-Lam. Buddhist Society.

The Light of Asia, Sir Edwin Arnold. Routledge 1971.

Mumonkan, tr. with commentary R. H. Blyth. Hokuseido Press 1966.

The Secret of the Gold Flower, tr. Wilhelm, commentary C. G. Jung. Kegan Paul 1931.

Selected Sayings from the Perfection of Wisdom, tr. Edward Conze. Buddhist Society 1968.

Some Sayings of the Buddha, tr. Woodward. Buddhist Society 1974.

The Tao Te Ching, tr. Chu Ta-kao. Buddhist Society.

The Voice of the Silence, H. P. Blavatsky. Theosophical Publishing House.

ON MEDITATION

Concentration and Meditation, Christmas Humphreys. Robinson and Watkins 1973.

Cutting Through Spiritual Materialism, Chögyam Trungpa. Robinson and Watkins 1973.

Meditation in Action, Chögyam Trungpa. Stuart and Watkins 1969.

The Practice of Recollection, Mangalo Bhikkhu. Buddhist Society.

POETRY

Any anthology of the great masters and of well-known poems.

Buddhist Poems, Christmas Humphreys. Allen and Unwin 1971.

OTHER WORKS

The Field of Zen, D. T. Suzuki. Buddhist Society 1969.

From Darkness to Light, Victor Gollancz. Gollancz 1964.

Karma and Rebirth, Christmas Humphreys. Murray 1942.

The Key to Theosophy, H. P. Blavatsky. Theosophical Publishing House 1946.

The Mahatma Letters to A. P. Sinnett, ed. Trevor Barker. Section III 'Probation and Chelaship'. Theosophical Publishing House 1923.

The Perennial Philosophy, Aldous Huxley. Chatto 1969.

Psychology and Religion, C. G. Jung. Yale University Press 1938.

Studies in the Middle Way, Christmas Humphreys. Curzon 1976.

Walk On!, Christmas Humphreys. Buddhist Society.

A Western Approach to Zen, Christmas Humphreys. Allen and Unwin 1972.

An Introduction to Zen Buddhism, D. T. Suzuki. Rider 1969.

The Yoga of the Bhagavad Gita, Sri Krishna Prem. Stuart & Watkins 1969.

FICTION

OM, Talbot Mundy. Hutchinson.

Sheldon Press books of related interest

THE SOUND OF THE ONE HAND
281 Zen Koans with Answers

Translated by Yoel Hoffmann
Foreword by Zen Master Hirano Sōjō

For the first time the mysterious exchanges which take place between a Zen Master and his student can be understood by the English-speaking reader.
281 paradoxical koans which the Zen Masters use to guide their pupils to enlightenment are given with their answers and an explanatory commentary.

THE WAY OF ALL THE EARTH
An Encounter with Eastern Religions

JOHN S. DUNNE
Introduction by Geoffrey Parrinder

'This book is meant for the general reader, to conduct him through a spiritual Odyssey and show the many illuminations that come on the way out and back.'
GEOFFREY PARRINDER

'No one could read it without being enriched by the range of ideas and experience to which it introduces one.'
JOHN A. T. ROBINSON

Books published by Sheldon Press

Afanas'ev Aleksandr, *Russian Fairy Tales*

Baelz, Peter, *Ethics and Belief*: 'Issues in Religious Studies'

Baker, Roger, *Binding the Devil*

Blum, Carol, *Diderot: The Virtue of a Philospher*

Branston, Julian, *The Story Teller: Poems*

Chen, Jack, *Inside the Cultural Revolution*

Clissold, Stephen, *The Wisdom of the Spanish Mystics*

Cragg, Kenneth, *The Wisdom of the Sufis*

Cupitt, Don, *The Leap of Reason*: 'Studies in Philosophy and Religion' 4

Cupitt, Don, *The Worlds of Science and Religion*: 'Issues in Religious Studies'

Donovan, Peter, *Religious Language*: 'Issues in Religious Studies'

Dunne, John S., *The City of the Gods*

Dunne, John S., *A Search for God in Time and Memory*

Ehrenzweig, Anton, *The Psychoanalysis of Artistic Vision and Hearing*

Fairlie, Henry, *The Spoiled Child of the Western World*

Fowler, David C., *The Bible in Early English Literature*

Frith, Nigel, *The Legend of Krishna*

Harrold, Charles F., *A Newman Treasury*

Hauck, Paul, *Overcoming Depression*

Hebblethwaite, Brian, *Evil, Suffering and Religion*: 'Issues in Religious Studies'

Hick, John, ed., *Truth and Dialogue*: 'Studies in Philosophy and Religion' 2

Holm, Jean, *The Study of Religions*: 'Issues in Religious Studies'

Holmer, Paul L., *C. S. Lewis: The Shape of His Faith and Thought*

Kelen, Betty, *Confucius*

Kopp, Sheldon, *If You Meet the Buddha on the Road, Kill Him!*

Kraemer, William, ed., *The Forbidden Love*

Leech, Kenneth, *A Practical Guide to the Drug Scene*

Leech, Kenneth, *Soul Friend*

Leech, Kenneth, *Youthquake*

LeShan, Lawrence, *Alternate Realities*

Lottman, Herbert R., *How Cities Are Saved*

Maclaren, Elizabeth, *The Nature of Belief*: 'Issues in Religious Studies'

McCulloch, Joseph, *Under Bow Bells*

Merton, Thomas, *The Asian Journal of Thomas Merton*

Merton, Thomas, *Conjectures of a Guilty Bystander*

Merton, Thomas, *The Monastic Journey*

Merton, Thomas, *The Power and Meaning of Love*

Merton, Thomas, *The Seven Storey Mountain*

Merton, Thomas, *The Sign of Jonas*
Merton, Thomas, *The Silent Life*
Merton, Thomas, *Thomas Merton on Zen*
Merton, Thomas, *The Waters of Siloe*
Merton, Thomas, *The Wisdom of the Desert*
Moffitt, John, *Journey to Gorakhpur*
Moreno, Antonio, *Jung, Gods and Modern Man*
Parrinder, Geoffrey, *African Traditional Religion*
Parrinder, Geoffrey, *Africa's Three Religions*
Parrinder, Geoffrey, *Asian Religions*
Parrinder, Geoffrey, *Bhagavad Gita: A Verse Translation*
Parrinder, Geoffrey, *Comparative Religion*
Parrinder, Geoffrey, *Jesus in the Qur'an*
Parrinder, Geoffrey, *Mysticism in the World's Religions*
Parrinder, Geoffrey, *Upanishads, Gita and Bible*
Parrinder, Geoffrey, *The Wisdom of the Forest*
Parrinder, Geoffrey, *Worship in the World's Religions*
Powell, Enoch, *No Easy Answers*
Pruyser, Paul, *Between Belief and Unbelief*: 'Studies in Philosophy and Religion' 3
Rajneesh, Bhagwan Shree, *No Water, No Moon*
Ramsey, Ian, *Christian Empiricism*: 'Studies in Philosophy and Religion' 1
Ringgren, H. & Ström, A. V., *Religions of Mankind*
Ross, Shirley, *Fasting*
Rowe, Andrew, *Democracy Renewed*
Sales, Grover, *John Maher of Delancey Street*
Scott, Carolyn, *Westminster Abbey: Its Links with the Famous*
Sidel, Ruth, *Women and Child Care in China*
Smith, Margaret, *Introduction to Mysticism*
Smith, Margaret, *The Way of the Mystics*
Stacey, David, *Interpreting the Bible*: 'Issues in Religious Studies'
Trigg, E. B., *Gypsy Demons and Divinities*
Unterman, Alan, *The Wisdom of the Jewish Mystics*
Way, Robert, *The Garden of the Beloved*
Weinberg, George, *Know Yourself, Help Yourself*
Willey, Fred, *The Honourable Member*
Zaehner, R. C., *The Teachings of the Magi*